INITIATIVE
AND
MANAGERIAL
POWER

INITIATIVE AND MANAGERIAL POWER

RAYMOND F. VALENTINE

amacom

A DIVISION OF AMERICAN MANAGEMENT ASSOCIATIONS

International standard book number: 0-8144-5315-5
Library of Congress catalog card number: 72-91060

First printing

*
To my sister Jo

PREFACE

Administrative power turns the wheels of progress in a business organization. A company cannot move forward unless the authority to handle its affairs, to make plans and decisions, and to manage people exists at all managerial levels. Formally delegated authority is certainly significant as a source of energy, but effective power is also found in unexpected places and unusual forms within the organization.

This book is addressed to all who exercise authority and to all who are in a position to delegate it. This includes everyone in management, from the top executive to first-line supervisors. It should be of interest to many outside the managerial class as well—for example, those who hope to reach the ranks of management and nonmanagers who nevertheless have power to influence plans and actions in a significant way. The book will be especially helpful to the reader who has a strong urge to increase his contribution to the company by legitimately exercising authority that lies dormant, unused, and therefore unproductive.

Considerable attention is given here to methods of increasing the effectiveness of the more orthodox means of delegating authority. But we must also look beyond the well-established, conventional approach to the distribution of authority; such an approach, by itself, is just not good enough to cope with current organizational realities. Thus a substantial portion of the book is devoted to a realistic consideration of an emerging concept for intensive and profitable distribution of power: the acquisition of authority through the initiative of the manager, without benefit of management's prior blessing.

The topics covered here are as relevant and practical as tomorrow's in-basket; they deal with forces that shape decisions, cause work to be done, and lead to improved performance. It is hoped that the discussion and case examples will provide additional personal insight into how to delegate, acquire, and use authority in a beneficial way. Pertinent techniques are explained and illustrated.

Like some other elements of the manager's job, the delegation of authority is part science, part art. That dual aspect is reflected in these chapters. Widely applicable, useful principles and procedures are discussed. The book describes concepts that the reader may come to believe in and want to absorb and modify for use within his own company's authority framework. Regardless of the specific design of the power structure that exists, the important point is that the delegation and acquisition of authority can be a positive process for improving company performance.

Raymond F. Valentine

CONTENTS

1 * INTRODUCTION

Authority—the power to command people and events—is a force that man covets, by his very nature. We prize authority not only for the pleasurable feeling of strength and control it produces, but for the material rewards it can provide. We cannot help being conscious of its presence because every one of us is subject to some form of authority.

In business, authority is the oldest function still recognized as being essential to successful joint performance by a group of individuals. The well-being of an organization depends, to a great extent, on how effectively authority is used. In a practical, everyday sense, it is one of the primary resources of a company, in a class with men and money. Once established, it is a permanent asset that

□ Continually energizes the people who move an organization toward its goals.
□ Does not depreciate through hard usage.
□ Maintains its full potential even when occasionally abused.
□ Does not deteriorate from age or through passage from hand to hand down through the organization.

Despite the importance of authority, and a universal interest in it, it is not exactly the most popular function within an organization. While we may understand the need for it, and even crave it for ourselves, we feel an element of uneasiness in the presence of power. Those who possess it are aware that they are accountable for its proper use. Those who are subject to it are never sure how they will be affected the next time the boss exercises his authority.

There is a challenging operational aspect to the use of authority. When authority is used to move people to do things, it becomes meaningful. But the man who has the authority to get things done must be able to make decisions as to just what things need doing, and how they are to be done. He must know enough about the technical aspects of the situation to avoid stepping into an ever present trap: successful management of people in doing the *wrong* things.

In recent years, authority has become the target of increasing criticism. Suspicion regarding the motives of those in authority has resulted in demands for increased limitations on the free-wheeling use of administrative power. The current rage against the Establishment and the Corporate State is merely the most recent aspect of this continuing trend. A variety of highly sensitive economic, social, and political factors have inevitably influenced the manner in which authority is used in the organization. A common phenomenon resulting from this situation is the effort by many corporations to mask the strength and dominance of the official power structure. Others—perhaps with something less than sincere motives—have turned to a variety of techniques for encouraging participative management.

Reaction to widespread criticism is only one major factor that has recently affected the way in which authority is exercised in business. The nature of the typical organization has undergone a drastic revision in the past 50 years, and the use of authority has had to be adapted to that as well. This is not just a matter of growth in the average-size enterprise; the changes have affected enterprises of all sizes. The significant changes include greater dependence on specialization in crafts and professions, increased mobility of managers, less stability in the working force, less reliance on a small number of dominant executives, more diffused contact between superiors and subordinates because of layering in the organization structure, and broadening of product lines and services.

A prominent and widely mentioned effect of these changes is the emergence of a pronounced feeling of impersonality in the enterprise. Whereas personal power was once a highly visible factor in the management of most companies, today it is no longer found to be a predominant, evident characteristic in the profile of the organization itself —even though the urge for power is still natural in the individual.

The style in which authority is exercised in business has undergone considerable change, too. It is more circumspect, more subdued. Authority is not talked about openly and candidly, as are other primary functions of the enterprise; and what we do hear about it is frequently stated in academic or critical terms.

It is the contention here that people in business have overacted to these apparently unfavorable changes relating to the use of authority. *Authority is being exercised much more modestly and tentatively than is necessary or desirable under current circumstances.* The factors that have outmoded the traditional manner of exercising authority will continue to have their effect—and, indeed, may go even further in the new direction. In recognition of this, we must adapt to the current situation and find suitable and effective ways to apply authority, which is such an important asset of a company.

What effect has the changing nature of authority had on the practice of delegation? Delegation, like authority, is hardly a new idea in management. Its history can be traced to the earliest forms of organization, as far back as those of biblical times. Unlike authority, however, which until recent years has been a stable and respected concept, the practice of delegation has probably always posed serious difficulties. Perhaps this is so because basic human traits often are in conflict with the act of delegation. Giving up one's authority to a subordinate is by no means a completely natural act; having contrived to secure it, our instinct is to hold on to it, even though we may concede to the logic that the delegation of authority will result in benefits.

Another basic attitude in opposition to delegation is our tendency to underestimate the ability of our juniors to exercise authority prudently. Allied to this is the inclination to overestimate the magnitude of the risks involved in possible errors of judgment by less experienced subordinates. Such bias often leads to excessively rigid control and the absence of a climate that encourages vigorous use of delegated authority.

In the days when an enterprise was dominated by a few powerful men, their reluctance to delegate authority in depth did not seriously hamper the organization's effectiveness. But in today's typical company, inadequacies exist in the process of delegation that tend to magnify the harmful effects of an impersonal climate and indifference to ambition often found in the enterprise. In spite of the increasingly unprofitable impact of poor delegation, it appears to be true, nevertheless, that few (if any) companies have a natural, inherent drive to stimulate the employees' acquisition and use of authority. Therefore, if administrative power is to be harnessed at an efficient level, management must cultivate and nurture a constructive pattern for the delegation of authority. Only deliberate action in this direction can satisfy the urge for power in individual members of the group and provide effective channels for the use of delegated authority.

If we measure the effectiveness of authority by the same yardsticks that are applied to other kinds of company resources, it is evident that authority is not used productively at a rate anywhere near its potential. Many companies have a distressingly large reservoir of untapped power in the form of *underutilized* authority. This does not refer to authority that is hampered by any social, economic, or legal limitations; its use would be perfectly acceptable in those terms. The principal reason for the existence of underutilized authority is the lack of a positive approach to the *delegation* of authority.

When authority is viewed as a resource, it becomes evident that the benefits produced by it will vary according to the effectiveness with which it is distributed and used down through the various levels of the organization. It is productive in direct proportion to the extent that it finds its proper place in the company structure and is exploited at that location. Yet it is a painful reality that many companies are faced with an incongruous situation: While large segments of potential authority lie unused, many capable managers stand ready to use it for the benefit of the company, but are deprived from doing so. The result is that profits are unrealized and managers are unfulfilled.

Relatively few companies utilize authority aggressively and creatively as a productive resource. The more obvious practice is the traditional (and often inflexible) one of formal delegation of authority that closely follows the lines of the organization structure. The principal product of this philosophy is *supervisory authority,* the power to be the boss over one's subordinates. Behind this official framework, there is often an informal organization structure, which may be quite extensive. It is usually unobserved and uncontrolled by management, following its own rules, and frequently conflicting with company goals. The informal organization is a loose and fluid set of relationships among employees, an arrangement usually concerned with generating enough power to get something specific accomplished, whereupon it changes its structure.

Severe limitations on the effective use of authority occur when management depends solely on delegation via the formal organization structure. By its very nature, this practice precludes taking advantage of many profitable opportunities that can arise from a more personal and objective concept of authority. And little is gained—in terms of increased profit—from the operation of an *informal* organization that is permitted to create sporadic surges of power without management guidance or interest.

Those who feel that a strictly organizational approach to delegation is inevitable, for lack of anything better, can take heart. Methods do exist whereby substantial portions of authority can be distributed in response to the initiative of managers, at locations in the company that permit effective application of discrete elements of authority.

Here are some basic reasons why authority often is not delegated in a positive and personalized way.

Formal authority is usually delegated in accordance with organization structure. (This is the company structure as visualized and approved by top management. It may be portrayed in chart form, or simply be understood by everyone to be the approved organization.) It is a basic and logical form of distribution, since the organization structure is commonly used to divide the tasks and personnel of the company into manageable components (such as departments and sections). The supervisor of each component is then delegated the authority to manage his subordinates in accomplishing his functions. (This was defined earlier as supervisory authority.)

Fundamentally, it is a perfectly reasonable approach to the distribution of authority. However, if delegation is oriented *totally* to the organization structure, underutilization of potential authority is bound to occur. The structure is relatively inflexible and static; changes in it occur slowly, whereas circumstances often require that authority be realigned quickly. The organization structure operates almost entirely in a vertical plane and through a limited number of channels. It is designed so that authoritative contact between people is made up and down the organization. In actual practice, however, it is frequently essential that some forms of authority be exerted horizontally, diagonally, and in a multitude of other directions.

Undeniably, the organization structure is an acceptable and useful means for distributing responsibility and delegating the basic elements of authority. But even though the structure provides a stable framework for the company, it cannot be regarded as a complete portrait of the enterprise. Viewed alone, it presents a false picture of order and clarity in the division of tasks and definition of responsibilities. The fact is that daily operations in most companies are dynamic and complex. Some provision is needed for flexibility in the application of authority to cope with constantly changing situations. Even when this need is recognized, however, the conclusion often is that it is too difficult to define and realign authority to meet each new shifting set of conditions. Consequently, officially delegated authority remains essentially general and static. The need for flexibility is therefore satisfied via the *informal* organization, in which the actual

6

distribution of power is often unknown to management. *Describing responsibility is easier, and more acceptable, than describing authority.* The most common practice in assigning a manager to a job is to state his responsibilities (for functions, tasks, or results), inform him of his authority to manage the people who will help him meet his responsibilities, and describe the limits on his authority ("You can't do this or that"). The missing vital ingredient is a description of the authority that he *can* exercise, over and beyond the basic supervisory authority he has over his subordinates.

It is a simpler matter to describe responsibilities—in a specific and assured way—than it is to describe authority. The risk of overlaps or conflicts between positions is more easily avoided. Responsibility lends itself to being pictured in terms of functions and tasks; delegated authority does not. Having described a manager's responsibilities, the need to define his power is neatly (but inadequately) handled by indicating that authority is delegated to the extent necessary to carry out his responsibilities.

To an increasing extent, authority is a dirty word and responsibility is a clean word in today's climate. The term "authority" is frequently used in a context implying that it is the cause of despotism and lack of freedom. We use nicer substitutes for the word and tend to avoid talking about authority as such, except in generalities.

As a consequence of this trend, there is a growing confusion between the words "responsibility" and "authority." People talk about the responsibilities of a position as though that suffices to describe the authority involved. It is ironic that while authority is almost an inflammatory word, the strong personal urge to acquire this power to make desirable things happen is still alive and well, and living in all of us.

The most practiced mode of leadership is to observe closely what subordinates are doing with their delegated authority and to offer advice freely. A final basic reason why authority often is not delegated in a positive way is related to leadership *style*. Almost every executive and supervisor is sure to state sincerely that he believes strongly in the delegation of authority. Moreover, he can "prove" that he

7

practices his belief. This is not difficult to do, since the organization structure provides for the distribution of authority in any case. But his claim may be meaningless, since the man who delegates the authority also has the role of a leader. Many managers choose to fulfill leadership by over-controlling their subordinates' activities on a detailed basis.

The reasons for this are numerous. The organization structure itself stimulates a bureaucratic and conservative attitude toward the use of authority. This attitude tends to encourage conformance and to discourage ingenuity in the use of delegated power. The boss may feel that his role is to insure that proper respect to past precedent and current policy is given by subordinates in exercising their authority. A more personal reason is that the typical boss is very conscious of the weight of his responsibility. To make certain he will not be criticized for errors made by his subordinates, he may choose to observe and closely control the authority he has delegated so that it will be used "correctly." Then, too, there is the boss who delegates authority in a limited way out of fear that powerful subordinates can usurp his authority to the point where he would be unable to control their activities—thus reflecting on his capabilities as a leader.

This book seeks to demonstrate that acceptable means are available for improving the practices used in delegation of authority, and for employing delegated and acquired power as a resource for better management and higher productivity. All this can be achieved by supplementing traditional principles with a flexible and personalized approach to the distribution of authority.

It is hoped that the reader will come to accept these concepts of authority as valid and useful in business today:

Authority produces benefits for the company only to the extent that it is used. Unused authority is like no authority at all, in terms of results. Furthermore, when potential authority (which would be productive if it were used) is allowed to lie dormant, it represents losses to the company that can never be regained.

Far less use is made of authority than is possible and acceptable under present conditions. We know that authority cannot be exercised in the uninhibited fashion of 50 or 100 years ago. But far greater productive use of authority can be made than many people in business seem to think is possible under current conditions. It is within the control of the enterprise to change many factors that cause underutilization of authority.

Distribution of authority must be related to the organization structure, but should not be limited by it. The organization basically gains its strength from the way in which authority is distributed to its various levels and components. The organization structure, however, has a high degree of inertia and inflexibility. Use of organization as the sole basis for controlling distribution of authority will substantially dilute the company's potential power. In a mature company, it is sometimes better to let the pattern of authority lead rather than follow the organization structure. Furthermore, when great emphasis is placed on delegation of authority according to the company's structure, the tendency is to give undue attention to *supervisory authority* (the power to manage people). This inhibits effective and productive use of two other basic types of authority: *operational authority* (the power to manage affairs so as to get things accomplished) and *commitment authority* (the power to make agreements with others for joint action).

Effective use of authority is gained by a combination of delegation and permissive acquisition of authority. The specific delegation of authority that is oriented to the organization structure and company policy provides management with basic control of the enterprise's operation and goals. This type of delegation should not set outside limits on the use of authority. Techniques of distribution and control should be designed to permit authority to operate within a flexible framework. Management must encourage and allow motivated personnel to use their initiative to assume (or acquire) authority that is insufficiently delegated to those points in the organization where it can be used most effectively. Acquired authority is that which is gained or taken for oneself by one's own efforts and actions, and which is then put to use. Hopefully, it is authority that does not rightfully belong to someone else, and that will be put to use constructively for the benefit of the company.

An effective means for adding reality to the delegation of authority (and encouraging the assumption of authority) is to tie it to achievement of company goals. The manager who understands and believes in the current goals of the company can (with guidance) construct a set of personal objectives, which he visualizes as relating directly to company goals. On the basis of personal objectives, specific statements of delegated authority can be developed; and areas can be outlined in which the manager can seek to expand his contribution through the *assumption* of authority. This approach provides a basis for

□ Realism in the use of authority.
□ Acquisition of a significant degree of power.
□ Encouragement to use initiative for sound expansion of authority without unnecessarily restrictive rules.

Control of the use of authority is necessary. Effective control can be achieved by a variety of means, not all of which need be "tight." The most meaningful and useful control methods are those that are inherent in existing systems, programs, or procedures and that are in existence for some other purpose. Usually, systems designed specifically and solely for control of authority are unnecessary and costly. Control of delegated authority should be tailored to the types of authority being monitored; varying techniques and degrees of control should be used. It is wasteful and inhibiting to subordinates if all controls are on a tight basis. There is no essential difference between the controlling of assumed authority and the controlling of formally delegated authority.

Since authority can be delegated and used at virtually all levels in the company, a clarification of the terms used to describe relationships between people at different levels should be helpful here. The words *boss* and *subordinate* indicate the relationship between men at two adjacent levels in the organization. And it is understood that the man who is a boss or superior in one relationship can also be a subordinate in another.

2 * TRADITIONAL VIEWS ON DELEGATION OF AUTHORITY

The benefits to be derived from delegation of authority were recognized long ago. Among the most active delegators were heads of organizations that were capable of generating massive power and profiting handsomely from effective use of it. Monarchies, religious groups, and military organizations were extremely efficient in practicing the art of delegation.

We continue to accept the ancient premise that authority is power arising from ownership. Authority grows from the act of committing talent or capital to the creation of an enterprise. These and other principles, to be discussed in this chapter, are still visible in practice today. It is also quite evident that the two basic types of authority structures—*line* and *staff*—which have been applied and refined over the centuries, remain the most prevalent forms in current use.

THE EXPANDABILITY OF AUTHORITY

The most striking characteristic of authority is that it can be multiplied by the act of delegating it to others. Although this feature has significant advantages, it also causes complications, as we shall see. Nevertheless, this trait of expandability makes authority a unique asset, a resource of great potential.

The principals of a company acquire their authority by

ownership. Suppose, however, they do not wish to run the company personally. They can hand over their authority, by delegation, to the top executive of the business. Even with this action, they still hold the ultimate authority. The top executive then divides his authority and parcels it out to subordinates throughout the entire structure of the company. Again, he, too, retains the full range of executive authority given him by the principals. Authority, then, is a right resulting from ownership and retained by the investors, who can simultaneously multiply it by delegating it to other people —at successively lower levels in the organization—who use it to operate the business.

WHY AUTHORITY IS DELEGATED

If a man can personally put to use the total potential of his authority, he has no need to delegate it. The need arises because the person who has the power is, for some reason, unable to make full use of it himself. This is a key point. Authority is power that generates activity to produce profit for a company. However, authority is effective only to the extent that it is used. If the man who has the power cannot use it fully, he should delegate it to subordinates who, by reason of their number and capabilities, *can* do so.

We sometimes encounter the narrow view that authority should be delegated only to individuals within the ranks of management. An essential fact is overlooked in such an approach. Many forms of authority, particularly those pertaining to making decisions and initiating action, can be delegated effectively down to the employee level. For many functions, delegation to submanagement levels permits fuller utilization of potential authority. The benefits that resulted from specialization by craft or profession would not have been possible if specialization did not include the delegation of authority to carry out specific actions.

CONTROL OF DELEGATED AUTHORITY

Delegation is the act of entrusting power to someone, who then performs as his boss's representative in using that authority. It is understood by all that, despite the delegation, the boss's authority remains intact and overriding. From this dual condition—giving away authority, yet retaining it—has evolved that useful (though sometimes troublesome) concept known as control. Control techniques permit the boss to remain aware of the way in which (his) authority is being managed by the subordinate. The availability of control techniques encourages the boss to parcel out his authority to subordinate managers. These methods, on the other hand, can be a burden to the subordinate, who realizes that the boss can use the controls to look over the manager's shoulder at any time, and even override the manager's decision if he sees fit.

THE PRESENCE OF RESPONSIBILITY

What is the price of power? One of the truisms about authority is that one must pay for having it by being responsible for exercising it correctly. The person who has authority is obliged to account for how he has used it—or failed to use it. On the face of it, this seems to be a fair exchange.

A related axiom is that the man who has the responsibility for doing something should have the authority to control whatever resources are needed to carry out his responsibility. It is unfair to require a man to accomplish an objective while limiting his power over the tools needed to do the job.

These traditional views of the relationship between authority and responsibility are still widely preached. However, they present an oversimplified version of what takes place in actual everyday business practice. The authority-responsibility relationship is obviously a significant factor in effective delegation. This does not necessarily mean that the two go hand in hand, or that they coexist in equal proportions. Actually, in many situations, authority and responsibility appear to be inconsistent. The relationship does not always portray a neat, formula approach. Although some of this inconsistency is deliberate and planned, more often it is not. Interaction with responsibility is one of the least understood, least explored aspects of authority (as is shown here in subsequent discussion).

CAN RESPONSIBILITY BE DELEGATED?

Delegation of responsibility differs somewhat from delegation of authority. In fact, a few knowledgeable observers have gone so far as to disagree with the concept that responsibility can be delegated at all. However, it appears that this contrary view is based more on semantics than on principle, in that it revolves around the definition assigned to the word "delegated." From a practical standpoint, responsibility certainly can be delegated, in the sense that a subordinate is placed in the position of being answerable for the results produced by his exercise of power, and is subject to penalty in case of failure.

The difference between the two kinds of delegation is that when authority is granted to a subordinate by his boss, the latter can choose to forget about it and never exercise that authority himself. (We know, however, that he can recover that authority at will.) On the other hand, when a boss delegates some of his *responsibility,* he cannot, even for a moment, divest himself (in the eyes of *his* bosses) from any portion of the responsibility he placed on his subordinate. Although he has shifted it, he continues to carry the actual burden of responsibility. Just as he may look to his subordinate to answer for the manner in which the latter has exercised his power, his own bosses look to him. He remains fully and actively responsible for seeing to it that the authority delegated to him is exercised properly, whether by himself or by a lower-level manager.

While there is this difference, it is nevertheless true that both authority and responsibility can be delegated— meaning, in the common sense, they can be assigned by a boss to a subordinate.

COMMON REASONS FOR DELEGATING AUTHORITY

Generally, people who hold power are willing to delegate at least some part of it. There are many reasons, a few of which are stated here in simple terms. (There are obviously many variations and exceptions even to these widely applicable, basic reasons.)

The man or men at the top (who hold the entire range of

authority) cannot personally superintend the detailed execution of their directives as the organization grows. By delegating portions of its authority, top management is better able to exercise overall control of the company. It is simply a matter of the physical and mental limitations that apply to all men, even the most powerful. The top managers in a company have a finite span of attention. Each can work just so many hours a day, and be in only one place at a time. As the volume of activity in an organization increases, management delegates larger and larger segments of authority.

Sheer size of the workforce is a basic reason for delegating authority. When an executive has more subordinates reporting to him than he can effectively manage, it is common practice to create an intermediate level of organization. The executive then parcels out segments to these new managers, taken from his bank of authority.

The competitive necessity for having specialists in the company is another important reason. Practically all business organizations employ a variety of specialists in various trades and professions. A specialist is valuable because he usually knows more than his boss about the specific field involved and can effectively put his knowledge to use, given the authority. Such delegation leaves the executive free to manage operations at a higher and broader level.

The very act of constructing a hierarchy, with layers of executives and supervisors, necessitates the delegation of authority. Management's willingness to do so is an important key to building a successful organization structure. Even beyond this, the process of subdividing functions and tasks in an enterprise requires that authority be distributed.

The fact that it is an outstanding means for developing people at all levels in the organization is a common and important reason for delegating authority.

COMMON DIFFICULTIES ENCOUNTERED
IN DELEGATING AUTHORITY

As in any major function of management, problems arise in the delegation of authority. Some of the ordinary difficulties encountered are cited here.

Knowing what goes on. The man who delegates authority to his subordinates comes to realize that his own bosses, while understanding the desirability of pushing authority down the organization, expect him to know in detail what goes on at the lower levels. It is the outgrowth of a practical fact: The act of delegating creates a need for the boss to maintain adequate knowledge and control of the use of that authority by his subordinates. Unfortunately, it is not always easy for the boss to maintain a fine balance between these two apparently conflicting requirements—his need to delegate authority and his responsibility for knowing how it is being used.

Having controls available. Related to the foregoing problem is the fact that adequate controls over the use of delegated authority are sometimes hard to come by. Methods are needed to warn of impending difficulties that may result from the subordinates' inadequate or improper actions. But the boss may find that available methods of control are so cumbersome and time-consuming, delegation sometimes does not seem worthwhile.

Passing information down the line. The subordinate, if he is to exercise his authority properly, often has a need for certain information to be passed along by his boss. Perhaps because of difficulties in communicating, the information is not always forthcoming; or perhaps the boss simply has no effective way of knowing which specific bits of information should be passed along.

Imposing personality problems. Personality problems frequently come into play in the process of delegating authority. There is the manager who simply will not let go of his authority, even after going through the motions of delegating it. He may be the type who prefers to deal with the substance and detail of the job rather than to manage the work of others. And so he hovers over those to whom he has supposedly delegated authority. Then there is the boss who came up the ranks himself, and who does not know how, or is afraid, to break away from his earlier pattern of running things himself.

The attitudes of subordinates can also cause difficulties. Some managers strongly resist using the entire range of authority granted to them. It may be because of a feeling of inadequacy, or lack of motivation, or simply because the manager feels he will be overburdened if he uses all his authority. This kind of resistance is especially noticeable in the case where management has not shown itself to be receptive to new ideas and there is a pattern of excessive penalties for mistakes by managers.

Personality problems, as well as the absence of a healthy climate, sometimes lend credence to a favorite axiom of believers in strong central authority: You can push authority for decision making down the line, but it won't stay down.

Skipping levels. Good communication practices are essential for achieving a flexible approach to the use of authority. Some line executives, who ignore their immediate subordinate managers and make direct contact with personnel below that level, are apparently unconcerned about the resultant confusion.

Any direct action by an executive to issue orders or advice to people in levels below that of his immediate subordinate can undermine the latter's position. It can also result in conflicts between the actions of the executive and those of his subordinate. Unless all levels know what is going on, problems are inevitable. There should be some means for the manager who is being bypassed to know (1) that direct contact is being made, (2) that the substance of the discussion will be relayed to him, and (3) that he will be consulted when the authority delegated to him comes into play. The communications channels can be simply some uncomplicated method for informing intermediate supervisors on a before-the-decision basis, or—when contact involves the passage of information—even on an after-the-fact basis. But the question is, will the boss faithfully follow the method?

LINE AUTHORITY

The two traditional forms of delegated authority that stand out above others in terms of maturity and popularity are *line authority* and *staff authority*. Line authority is that which is delegated by the company's top executive to his immediate subordinates, who are charged with carrying out the operations of the company. These men in turn redelegate some of their power down the line of vertical authority to the next level. This is done in turn at each level until the first-level supervisor is reached. Line authority, then, is possessed by individual supervisors as a result of distribution throughout the organization of appropriate portions of the total authority held by the top man.

Line authority is the power that a manager has to direct the efforts of subordinates in the everyday performance of their assigned tasks. It gives him the right to make decisions applying to his operational area, and the power to enforce these decisions. It is the authority that makes a man "the boss" to his subordinates. Line authority also provides the principal channel for passing down orders to successively lower levels in the organization. By this means, there is a reasonable assurance that what has been ordered will be done, since the necessary power for enforcing the orders is in the hands of managers at each level.

How Line Authority Is Related to Company Structure
In theory, the official pattern of delegated line authority should coincide generally with the organization structure. Where this is the case, a man who is selected for a position in the organization acquires a ready-made package of delegated authority. In such event, it can be said that authority resides in the *position* rather than with the man. Each occupant, when he moves into the position, inherits that delegated authority. Of course, the scope and the intent of the original delegation can be changed deliberately by management, or they can be changed as a result of some incident, either accidental or calculated. As a matter of fact, there are usually many factors in operation that can cause the actual power structure in the company to be quite different from the formal organization structure as advertised. This divergence can cause a variety of effects, good and bad, including changes in the organization of the company to make it conform with the power structure rather than vice versa.

To visualize how line authority is delegated, it should be

remembered that all the people at any given level have less authority, together, than the total amount held at the next higher level. This is based on a practical concept that no man can ever delegate away *all* his authority, since he retains at least the power to recall whatever authority he has delegated at any time he deems it necessary.

The traditional pattern of delegated line authority can be portrayed graphically, if we visualize authority as "units" of power. The accompanying diagram shows that a total of 50 units has been delegated to the president (by the board of directors). The president can redelegate this authority, assigning a given number of units to each subordinate.

As indicated earlier, the units of authority at any horizontal level in the organization never add up to the total units held at the next higher level. Here, the president has delegated 15 units each to the three vice-presidents, for a total of 45 units. This means that he has retained 5 (undelegated) units of authority, representing his power to make certain

DISTRIBUTION OF UNITS OF POWER
IN A LINE ORGANIZATION

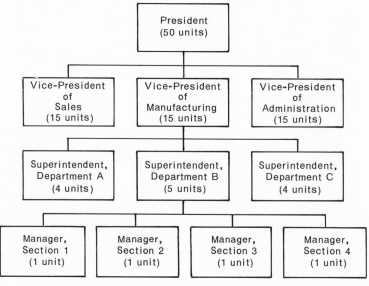

decisions reserved to the presidential level. Since he also retains ultimate control over the 45 units that he has delegated, he is credited with the entire 50 units.

At the next level, the vice-president of manufacturing has distributed his delegated authority in a similar fashion. He, however, deliberately has not distributed it evenly: The superintendent of Department B has 5 units, while the other two superintendents have 4 units each. (This, of course, does not mean that Superintendent B has authority over the other two, or that he is superior to them organizationally. But he *may* receive a higher salary.) The total delegated authority of the three department heads adds up to 13 units—two less than the total of 15 held by the vice-president of manufacturing. Thus we can visualize the hierarchy of authority. Each subordinate at each level has a share of the total authority in the company, but never do all the delegates at any level have a combined authority as high as that of the man above them.

STAFF AUTHORITY

Staff authority—also known as functional authority—is a form of power delegated to staff components in the organization. It is, for example, the right to carry out on behalf of top management specialized functions that are applicable to the entire organization. Although the man with staff authority has significant influence over specific activities in the company's everyday operations, he does not have direct control over them.

This characteristic is seen in some of the more common functions in which staff authority is found, such as personnel administration. The personnel department provides line supervisors with guidance and advice on selection, training, promotion, and discipline of employees, as well as many other personnel-oriented activities. Yet the line supervisors themselves usually make the actual decision regarding the personnel action. In the systems planning function, the staff department develops proposed systems or procedures, for example, but a line supervisor is under no obligation to put these proposals into effect until they are approved by a competent higher official who has line authority over him. A similar situation exists in budgeting—another common staff function—in which the staff group recommends, advises, and assists in the development of budgets by line components.

In larger companies, other types of staff functions are frequently assigned. Here, it is not unusual to find that staff authority is delegated to specialists at the corporate level, who advise on policy, planning, and control of major line functions, such as purchasing, marketing, and engineering.

Staff offices are not located in the vertical line between operating officials and lower levels, but are off on the side of the organization structure; and there is no one in line below them over whom they have direct power. Nevertheless, as specialists in administrative, technical, and operational functions, they do exert indirect control over line executives and supervisors at lower levels. The reason is that they have the power to recommend—to higher officials—policies and procedures that affect the way in which the lower line executives and supervisors exercise their authority.

How Staff Authority Is Distributed and Used
Whenever a line executive delegates authority to his staff, it represents some dilution of the authority of lower-level *line* officials. This occurs because line officials are governed by those staff-originated proposals that are approved by higher management. The advantages that a company realizes by delegating staff authority are substantial enough to offset the disadvantages that may result from limiting supervisors' authority. For instance, it is more feasible to acquire, through a staff organization, the degree of specialization needed for proper administration of certain functions. A common example is personnel administration, in which functions such as recruiting, negotiation, and training can be carried out more skillfully through participation by industrial relations specialists. These staff people carry out their authority in many helpful ways—advising line officials and supervisors, actually carrying out a function in whole or in part, or developing systems and procedures to be followed by line supervisors.

A considerable variety of functions, which could actually be carried out through line managers if the company so decided, are certain to benefit from the higher level of skill, knowledge of current practice, and concentration that is more readily available from staff specialists. These people focus their attention and efforts on relatively narrow fields. It is often unreasonable to expect line supervisors to have all the abilities needed to supervise specific processes. There may be need, too, for a high degree of standardized administration of certain tasks, a uniformity that would not be achieved if each line manager had the authority to administer tasks independently.

There is an economical limit to the amount of staff authority that can be delegated. Since it diminishes the authority of the line manager, there comes a point when the cumulative effect of delegation to staffs begins to seriously hamper the line manager's ability to manage. The extent and manner of distribution of staff authority is very much at the option of management. This contrasts sharply with line authority, in that it is just not possible to operate a company of any size without the delegation of line authority. It is at least theoretically possible not to have *any* delegation of staff authority in a company. In many companies, however, there is substantial delegation because of the availability and the benefits of specialization by functions.

There are not many advocates of the idea that a staff man should be assigned any degree of direct power over the line organization. Invariably, it is officially accepted that the channel of staff authority goes up, by way of a higher level of line authority, before the effects of staff power descend into the organization. In actual practice, the real effectiveness of the man with staff authority is measured by his ability to make things happen in the line organization. If he causes things to happen successfully often enough, he acquires real authority in the organization. The need for him to operate through official channels diminishes. His decisions and advice are respected down the line, and he is able to operate somewhat like an honorary member of the line organization. While this situation is subject to some abuse, it appears that the most effective use is made of skilled staff specialists when they are accepted by line people as members of the family.

3 * MODERN VARIATIONS OF DELEGATED AUTHORITY

Every era of management has its own needs and achieves its own refinements. This century has produced interesting variations of line and staff authority—which are still the predominant styles of delegation. The present state of the "art" of delegation can be fairly described in this way:

(1) Authority is still largely distributed by management on the basis of organization structure.

(2) There is less and less public and private reference, by businessmen, to the concepts of authority and even to the word "authority" (except in a derogatory sense). However, there is greater personal interest than ever, by individuals, in acquiring and using power in the organization.

(3) This century's innovations are largely a passive reaction to the need to adapt to powerful factors that have changed the character of the organization. These factors, such as increasing size and diversity, greater specialization in skills, and increasing mobility and turnover in work force, tend to depersonalize a company.

(4) No positive trend has emerged toward using delegation in a constructive way to increase the personal achievement of managers. Little use is made of techniques that can capitalize on authority as a significant resource.

The most apparent new twentieth century approaches to delegating authority can be classified under two headings: *decentralization,* which relies heavily on delegation via the organization structure, and *implied authority,* which departs somewhat from the traditional patterns in that it is not oriented to formal delegation along organizational lines.

DECENTRALIZED ORGANIZATION:
AN IMPORTANT INNOVATION

Use of decentralization has been an important factor in industrial growth in this century. The concept has made it easier for businesses to increase in size while retaining effective management at all levels. The principal characteristic of the decentralized enterprise is that it is subdivided into a number of separate organizations, each virtually independent in the management of daily operations, but all under strong control of the parent company in matters of major policy. The giant corporations in the automobile industry are prime examples.

Decentralization ranks as a major response to the administrative problems that arise from the increasing size of modern enterprises. Of particular interest to us, it emphasizes the usefulness of massive delegation of authority to major subordinate divisions within the organization. Each decentralized division of the parent corporation acts almost like a separate, independent company. Management in each division has the power to make and carry out a wide variety of very important decisions regarding its own operations. Like an independent company, it is judged on its performance and profits rather than on the characteristics of its managers.

In describing the action of a decentralized division as almost like that of a separate company, the word "almost" is very significant. The reservation arises from the fact that the parent corporation usually consists of a powerful superstructure designed to maintain a specific degree of control over vital aspects of the independent divisions. The superstructure maintains control by retaining for itself (that is, not delegating) the authority to make decisions on major policy matters. This permits the maintenance of broad but effective limits within which the subsidiaries must operate. Another means by which the parent company maintains its authority is by control of the financing of divisional operations. The corporation also reserves the right to hire and fire top executives in the divisions.

The decentralized organization, then, is characterized by extensive delegation of authority to the divisions for independent management of their operations, but with maintenance at the parent company level of central control of vital decisions. While operational authority is freely delegated, there remains a substantial degree of centralized power over the divisions, coupled with the ever present possibility of recalling or overriding delegated authority at the option of corporate management.

The Significance of Decentralization
Having been described earlier as a "passive reaction" to an impersonal factor, such as the increasing size of the enterprise, the decentralization technique would appear to be applicable only to giant corporations. In what way, then, is decentralization relevant to the goal of improved use of delegated authority?

The fact is, the way in which authority is delegated to the divisions in a decentralized organization can be useful in businesses of all sizes. This becomes evident when we examine the reasons why this concept evolved. The decentralized concept of organization owes its existence as much to what it can prevent as to what it can achieve. For example, it acts as an antidote for specific problems that can occur in practically any organization: inflexibility due to top-heavy management; the possibility of incorrect decisions by executives at too high a level in the organization (mistakes that may result because these people are not close enough to details that can be important in decision making); missed opportunities for effective action because of inability to make fast, accurate decisions at the working level.

It is interesting to note that the title commonly applied to this widely known concept of delegated authority is "decentralized organization." The second word is well chosen. The emphasis is on pushing power down the organizational chain to components of the structure (such as divisions of a corporation). We can speculate that if this concept were carried to a logical conclusion and moved several steps further down the structure to the level of the individual *manager,* we could validly use the phrase "decentralized *management"* instead. In that case, the benefits of decentralization could be stated on a much more personalized basis, as follows:

□ It promotes timeliness and clarity in decision making.

□ It places decision-making authority at the lowest managerial level capable of making proper decisions.

□ It decreases the potential for conflict among the various managers of the organization.

□ It satisfies the urge of good managers to act independently in their areas of competence.

□ It increases the availability of talented managers who are experienced in independent decision making and management of operations.

□ It allows for more democracy in management (an atmosphere especially prized by today's young people).

□ It provides opportunities for utilizing the expanding pool of talented personnel. These people are needed in order to deal with the increasing complexity involved in achieving successful operations, even in small organizational components.

THE RISE OF IMPLIED DELEGATION
OF AUTHORITY

In the search for greater flexibility in delegation and use of authority, a number of techniques have been used that do not follow the traditional concepts of delegation. These forms represent a breakaway from some of the limitations that exist when authority is delegated strictly in accordance with organization structure. Of the many variations in use, the four major types discussed here are program management, task groups, coordinators, and the use of formal written procedures.

Users of these techniques do not always recognize that they are employing them to avoid some restriction imposed by more formalized methods of delegation. Sometimes, in fact, it is not even recognized that delegation of authority is involved. In more sophisticated organizations, it is not uncommon to find the assignment deliberately stated in terms that ignore the presence of authority; rather, they speak of what is to be accomplished, or the means by which it will be accomplished, or perhaps the responsibilities of the manager involved. Often, much of the authority that exists in such situations is developed by strategic maneuvering, or simply by naked strength, whereby the man with the assignment seeks forceful recognition of his having some kind of effective power. It is apparent that a considerable amount of the power distributed by means of these techniques can more rightfully be described as *implied* authority rather than formally delegated authority.

Implied authority is power that is understood to exist without being openly and officially expressed. Its characteristics are significantly different from those of normally delegated authority. Since it is not asserted in the usual fashion, implied authority is less visible to others in the organization, and it may have to be demonstrated or proved in each new use of it. Even when authority is stated, but is assigned for a limited scope of activity or a fixed period of time, it is regarded as abnormal or transitory in the minds of some people in the organization. In general, authority granted in some manner other than the traditional forms of line and staff authority is regarded by many as being counterfeit or tricky in some way.

Authority that is implied, or is in unusual form, is not necessarily defective or disadvantaged. These forms of authority are apt and effective in certain circumstances; a more formal type of delegation might be impractical, unsound, or unwarranted. Most important, if this kind of delegation were not available, occasions would arise in which *no* form of distributed authority existed in instances where it was actually needed. Frequently, much is to be gained through an imaginative approach to delegating authority, by using unconventional modes that happen to fit the particular conditions of a situation.

Program Management

The title "program manager" is a generic term covering both "product manager" and "project manager." *Product* management has been in existence for many years, especially in companies engaged in the manufacturing and marketing of consumer goods. In exercising this concept, a newly developed product is assigned to an executive, who is then in charge of managing it to a point of maturity. He is particularly concerned with the advertising, distribution, marketing, and sales functions. To support his efforts, individuals are borrowed from these functional departments and assigned to him as a temporary team. (Some variations of product managers are "brand" and "market" managers, who similarly operate with a composite functional team for a defined period of time.)

A somewhat similar concept has been emerging in recent years with the use of *project* managers. Here, the assignment typically applies to the development of a hardware program, or some complex system, rather than to a consumer goods program. (The title "project manager" also has variations, such as "program manager." However, the latter term is used in a more generic sense. Program management refers to all those management stratagems whereby various disciplines and functions are brought together on a team basis to achieve a single major objective, usually within a specified period of time.)

The use of project managers has been prompted by the many benefits to be derived from organizing a multidisciplined team to push through the development and implementation of a major project. Such projects usually involve the efforts of many different departments, skills, contractors, or suppliers, which must be coordinated to achieve the end result. The aerospace industry has been prominent in the use of project managers to carry out massive programs for development, construction, and utilization of new aircraft and space vehicles or supporting systems. The military services have benefited greatly in using project managers to develop and implement complex weapon systems.

The *program* management approach represents an effort to solve a difficult and pervasive problem: how to retain the benefits of the classic "line" organization while seeking the benefits of having an assembled group of specialists from various components work as a team on a specific project— on a temporary or part-time basis. There are obvious advantages in an organizational device that provides an integrated team of specialists dedicated to a single objective; but there are also difficulties associated with establishing a place in the power structure for such a temporary group. In program management, it is almost always necessary for the group to expend a considerable amount of its strength in trying to reduce the inevitable abrasions that result from conflict between the two organizational concepts—the permanent line organization and the temporary program manager.

Authority for program managers. Despite extensive experience with program management in business enterprises, there is still a lack of conviction as to the kind of authority structure that permits effective use of this concept. One approach has been to maintain the usual range of functional departments in the organization, and then add one or more separate, permanent program management departments. Each program department has a wide range of functions. When a project assigned to the program management department has been carried to the point of maturity and becomes routinized, the project drops out of the program concept. The various aspects of the project may then migrate back to the respective specialized departments having normal responsibility for those functions. The program management department is then assigned a new project.

In companies that have a continuing need for men with techniques and functions that are highly oriented toward program management, the permanent organizational approach has been used successfully. Here, the nature and objectives of successive projects may change, but certain functional characteristics and management skill requirements persist. In such companies it makes eminently good sense to retain specialists in a permanent program department, where they are continuously available to apply their abilities to a succession of projects.

Often, however, program departments must contend with assignments that differ radically from one another. If the nature of the industry or organization is such that each project designated for program management has its own particular skill requirements and functional requirements, the department must be frequently restructured to meet these needs. Because of this problem, it is more typical in a business enterprise to find that the program manager and his team are organized on a temporary basis, completely outside the established organizational structure of the company.

Even in this team concept, the program manager is faced with inherent difficulties regarding the authority available to him. The team's goals cut across many permanent company functions. Therefore, the manager finds that the authority he requires is already doled out, in a splintered fashion, to many regular functional components of the company. In response to this problem, the authority structure needed to support program responsibilities may be hand-tailored by higher management over a period of time, as the specific needs for various kinds of power become evident. Or the program manager himself may hammer out the authority he feels is necessary to the job.

Typically, then, in program management there is little difficulty in spelling out the manager's responsibility. The end result he must achieve is relatively concrete and specific. But since the delegation of authority is beset with difficulties, authority often is not discussed or not suitably described. Again, the reason is evident: The program manager's task is superimposed on a full-blown organization structure, across which has been distributed the very functions the program manager must employ in carrying out his single project. So he must figuratively fight to acquire his authority by employing the responsibilities that have been given to him.

What options does a program manager have in trying to diminish the need to "fight for his life" while gaining adequate authority? Where possible, he should try to get a written charter covering his program authority; it should be a specific statement, approved by management, describing the program objectives, the manager's responsibilities, and the authority that is unquestionably his, even if it is rather limited. The primary purpose is to establish a power base from which the manager can continue to build the essential authority he needs.

If it is not possible to secure a written charter because of administrative or political reasons, the program manager must still seek to build a base of power himself. His best course of action is to start with his program responsibilities, which are usually evident, and analyze them. The manager then can draw conclusions as to the authority he needs for meeting those responsibilities. How, then, does he establish the right to exercise this authority? Generally, he does it in piecemeal fashion, building up his power base in steps. He may attempt to carry out an authoritative action and see what the reactions are. Or he may prepare a memo or letter for his boss's signature, establishing the fact that he is empowered to carry out some particular action, implying some degree of authority. By a succession of these segmented expressions of implied or delegated authority, the program manager gradually fills out his power framework.

Building authority in this way is sometimes a tedious process, but experience eventually shows how it can be accelerated. The most significant aid to the program manager in these circumstances is that there is usually a very large reserve of authority that has not yet been asked for by anyone else.

Task Groups
The establishment of a task group, or temporary committee, is a popular device (despite the old joke that "a camel is a horse put together by a committee"). It is most commonly used when management believes that no established component in the organization is able to solve a pressing problem or devise plans for a specific purpose. While it seldom occupies a line position in the organization, a task group nevertheless must have some authoritative stature in order to produce even an elementary result.

The manner in which authority is assigned to a task group is at times even more casual than in the case of a program manager. The emphasis is on results expected from the group and on its responsibilities. Authority is usually given in the form of a sweeping statement to the effect that the task group is authorized to employ a certain amount of its members' time, as well as the time of such other personnel as is necessary to gain the needed facts, and to engage in such other acts as are needed to accomplish the group's tasks. This type of delegation can be of little help to the group. It tends to confirm the opinion of those with whom it does business that the group is a nuisance, and is bound to interfere with the normal operations of the organization. However, it is usually recognized that the task group must be tolerated (though barely), even though it may duplicate responsibilities already permanently assigned to someone, who should have been made to do the task group's job in the first place.

A *standing committee* may fare better than a task group because its longer tenure provides more time to construct a power base. Because such committees are generally engaged in activities having no counterpart in the regular organization structure, they also reduce the degree of potential conflict of authority. Sometimes, if a standing committee has energetic members, it seizes the initiative to construct a pattern of authority that can be inferred from the committee's charter.

The question of who has the authority can provoke sharp jurisdictional conflicts between a task group and an established component in the organization. This is especially so when the disputed authority directly or indirectly parallels the delegated authority of a powerful component in the company. Regardless of whether the task group is involved in this sort of intramural warfare or has the more conventional problem of getting company people to react to its implied authority, there are generally two basic courses the group can follow.

First, the group can attempt to throw its weight around— either by carrying out authoritative actions and waiting for a reaction, or by having the superior who established the group declare that it has certain specific authority (possibly announcing this on an incremental basis).

Second, the group can negotiate with the heads of established components to seek recognition of its temporary authority. A good negotiating point for the task group is to volunteer to relinquish its authority when its temporary existence ends and turn it over to the permanent component.

Coordinators

The attempt to define the extent of his delegated authority can be a frustrating matter for a coordinator. Business organizations frequently find themselves in circumstances in which it is convenient for them to assign an individual or office as coordinator of a program or system, on either a temporary or continuing basis. The task assigned is usually in addition to those involved in the regular job. A coordinator is often used under this typical set of circumstances: Management wishes to have someone monitor or oversee a program in which a variety of different components or individuals participate. The coordinator is to make sure that the program moves on schedule, and that the various people involved are interrelating effectively. For some reason, however, management does not want to assign the monitoring task to an office or individual having line authority over the people carrying out the program. This absence of authority to order action is the basis of the coordinator's frustrations. He is seldom certain of the nature and extent of his delegated authority—if any.

It often seems to the coordinator as though he has all the responsibility for insuring that proper action is being taken, and none of the delegated authority to assist him in seeing that it gets done. In effect, when authority is needed to make something happen—even a very small thing—the coordinator must go to someone higher in the organization and explain why he wants him to use his higher authority. Of course, the higher official resents the coordinator's inability to make the program go without bothering him for help, and he may openly question the coordinator's ability to do his job by whatever means he has at his command.

The most helpful tool a coordinator can possess is an established and well-defined program with highly visible milestones or schedules. This should be coupled with a publicized expression of the tasks management has assigned to the coordinator and a description of his duties, including the essential responsibility for reporting delinquencies to

higher management. This opportunity to report progress—
and the lack of it, in the form of delinquencies—can become the coordinator's most powerful source of implied authority.

When he is initially "tested" by participants in the
program (through their lack of action, for example), if the
coordinator reports the delinquency and management
cracks down on the delinquent, the occurrence becomes
widely known and the coordinator's authority is established.
But it is also helpful if he can be influential in other ways
that do not depend on the fear of being put on report. For
example, the coordinator can gain influence and prestige
(which he can then bring to bear as a form of authority) by
being knowledgeable about the problems of participants
and providing them with practical ideas as to how to meet
their obligations. Or he can request designation of a specific individual in each participating department to serve as
a contact point for the program, and then use that person's
membership in the department for authority leverage.

It is essential that the coordinator arm himself with a variety of forms of implied authority. The reason, as he soon
learns, is that official authority is seldom delegated, since
outright delegation is really contrary to the concept of the
coordinator's role.

Implying Authority via Procedures

One of the most useful ways of distributing authority for
specific purposes is by the use of written procedures. (Procedures are normally a detailed expression of company policy, which itself is based on the way top management visualizes authority.) The advantage of this method is that
authority can be passed out in small packages, highly tailored to the specific needs of a situation. The judicious distribution of authority via a written procedure is one way of
encouraging more intensive use of available power. Unfortunately, it also has a serious disadvantage, since the very act
of being specific creates limits in the flexibility of the system. Thus it is frequently necessary to pass up the line, for
decision, a large volume of cases not covered in the
"book." This disadvantage can be minimized if the proce-

dure specifically grants permission to make decisions and take action in cases that deviate from the ordinary.

There are many benefits in using written, or even oral, procedures as a means of distributing authority. Authority can be specifically placed where it can be well handled. The procedural format affords a means for defining the scope of the implied authority. It is also a means by which authority can be safely handed down below the supervisory level, in cases where the capability exists. This serves to permit utilization of available talent in an organizational zone where there is usually an insufficient use of authority potential.

4 * ACQUIRED AUTHORITY: DELEGATION BY INITIATIVE

Line and staff authority will certainly continue to be primary concepts for distributing power in the organization because they are both useful and familiar. The more recent variations discussed in the last chapter will continue to be used, too, in a wide variety of applications. Nevertheless, there is an obvious need for new techniques for the distribution of authority. If we believe otherwise, it means that we are willing to accept an uneconomical situation presently existing in many companies; that is, a great deal of potentially profitable authority goes unused while, at the same time, serious problems resulting from badly distributed authority remain unresolved.

There are effective ways, which are relatively unknown, for delegating authority within conventional channels (to be discussed later). Of paramount interest at this point is the probability that many companies are now in a position to achieve a breakthrough in the effective application of available administrative power through the technique of *acquired authority*. This method promotes a far higher rate of utilization of authority than is currently experienced in most companies. It also permits the manager to achieve a greater degree of self-control over his participation in the affairs of the enterprise.

It has been said that each generation devises a mode of organization and a power style to fit its own vision of how things should be. If this is so, the concept of acquired authority may reach its deserved stature, for it is attuned to current trends toward participative management, the merger of personal objectives with company goals, and the humanizing of the corporate structure.

WHAT IS ACQUIRED AUTHORITY?

Acquired authority is the power that a manager gains by his own efforts and actions. Delegated authority is granted; acquired authority is taken. Despite this essential difference, the common objective of both is that authority will be put to constructive use for the company's benefit.

Although acquired authority is evidenced in practically every enterprise, rarely does a company deliberately set out to encourage and expand the use of it. A common case of acquired authority can occur when a man has developed a procedure that is used by personnel over whom he has no authority. Because he has attained knowledge through developing the procedure (and providing he retains an interest in it), he is looked upon as an expert. If he makes himself available to help implement the procedure and gives advice regarding the improvement of it, he can quickly acquire the equivalent of authority over that procedure and the people operating it. In such a situation, he can play the dual role of an official who approves the procedure (by making changes to facilitate implementation of it) and a first-line supervisor (by influencing employees as to the manner in which they carry out the procedure).

In most companies in which acquired authority is present, it exists in a very random, unproductive way, and usually by accident rather than as the result of deliberate policy. It is not generally recognized that a company has the option of deciding whether or not to actively encourage managers and supervisors to seek out opportunities to grasp power on their own initiative. To many executives, the very idea of such encouragement may sound like heresy. It may seem to them that this concept undermines the pillars of the organization, which is based on a foundation of delegated authority. Nevertheless, a number of companies have made the decision and have profited significantly by supplementing the regular distribution of authority with the practice of encouraging self-initiated acquisition of authority.

It is evident that acquired authority is not bad in itself. The risk of misuse can be minimized with adequate management control. As we shall see, it can become a powerful means for building profit, improving operations, and increasing the satisfaction of managers in terms of greater participation in company affairs. A deliberate program for sponsoring the acquisition of authority can provide a breakthrough to new ground in the effective utilization of potential authority.

AVAILABILITY OF ACQUIRED AUTHORITY

How is it possible for someone to acquire and exercise authority that has not been delegated to him? Where does it come from? By what right does he acquire it? Why should the use of acquired authority be encouraged?

To state it simply, authority exists because the company exists. Authority is there because talent and capital were invested in the creation of the enterprise, and because the enterprise has a purpose and a natural desire to achieve that purpose. Authority is present in the company, whether or not that power is ever put to use. When a company is formed, and as it develops, a pool of potential authority is created. The pool grows, diminishes, and varies as the company undergoes changes in size, objectives, functions, products or services, financial condition, and so on. Since authority has an independent existence of its own, regardless of the extent to which it is actually put to use, it is apparent that a company may be operating at a very low degree of utilization of its total range of available authority.

Clearly, therefore, management should take positive action to encourage the use of acquired authority. Otherwise, a very substantial amount of the available authority will remain dormant. The distinct role of acquired authority is that it provides an additional significant avenue for increasing the percentage of potential management power that can be used to good advantage.

Consider a typical authority pattern in a company, in terms of the distribution of total authority existing at a given time. Perhaps 35 percent of total potential power is formally delegated as line and staff authority. Another 15 percent is in use in the form of implied delegations, via program managers, coordinators, and the like. The remaining 50 percent will be used only if an individual takes the initiative to acquire it under unofficial circumstances. Where there is no positive encouragement by management to acquire authority, we find that this remaining 50 percent is divided into two parts: no more than 10 percent is actively in use because someone has assumed it, despite the handicaps; the remaining 40 percent lies dormant and unused.

Why is there so much unused authority in the typical company? Three principal reasons, related to the real-life aspects of authority discussed previously, are summarized here:

First, management usually does not perceive that it can take positive action to identify and assign most of the authority that can be used profitably.

Second, most of us possess a degree of those common human traits that tend to inhibit extensive delegation of authority—for example, fear of being held responsible for an error that might result from misuse of authority delegated to a subordinate, or fear that our position and stature will be diminished somehow by delegating away too much authority.

The third reason for unused authority is that traditional concepts of line organization continue to support a widespread conviction that it is dangerous to permit power to be distributed in an informal manner. The belief in management by strict lines of authority is bound to die very hard.

For those who would feel more comfortable about the concept of acquired authority if they could relate it to an accepted principle of good management, consider the doctrine of eminent authority. Every member of management has the right and obligation to act in a reasonable and even energetic fashion to protect the company's best interests, even when it means that he must exercise authority that has not been delegated to him. Since it is difficult to foresee all the circumstances in which a manager should take action, authority simply cannot be delegated or implied to cover every particular point that can possibly arise. Therefore, every manager should act to acquire authority when the circumstances are such that he is in a position to protect the company, or to take advantage of a situation on behalf of the company.

A competent manager understands that he is not inhibited from acting in the company's behalf simply because his boss has failed to take positive action to invest him with specific authority. As a member of management, the manager is an integral part of the organization. So it is his right and obligation to assume authority to carry out an action for the benefit of the company under favorable conditions—for example, when he is aware that no one else is doing so, and when he feels competent to exercise the authority, and when his action does not contravene the expressed policy and best interests of the company. Two basic instances in point are: a tempting bargain causes a buyer to exceed his contractual authority; a sales manager relaxes the company's prices or other sales terms (within legal limits) in order to get an exceptionally large order, even though he is not specifically empowered to offer such terms. It is not always easy for the man on the spot to decide whether or not there is sufficient justification to go ahead and assume the authority on his own initiative. But like other management skills, good judgment in this area can be developed through study and experience.

Some companies have gone a considerable way in encouraging the use of acquired authority. One division of a well-known international corporation has advertised this policy to its managers for years: "All authority not expressly (and in writing) reserved to higher management is granted to lower management." Under this concept, the decisions that a manager is not entitled to make within the scope of his functions are spelled out. For all other decisions, he can assume that he has the authority and responsibility. The premise is that each manager is given a broad area of authority. As a result, operational decisions have been pushed far down the organizational structure, as close as possible to the site of the action to which the decision applies.

THE KINDS OF AUTHORITY
THAT CAN BE ACQUIRED

The kinds of authority that managers can acquire—the types of power that are not delegated and are available for acquisition—do not fall into unique categories. There are no particular classes that are universally undelegated and unused. However, there are many types of authority situations in which it is common to find large amounts of potential authority lying dormant and ready for acquisition. This list of various kinds of authority to be acquired is by no means a complete one:

☐ The authority to demand of others, who are not subordinates, that they execute their responsibilities in order that the manager can do his job better.

☐ The authority to negotiate with peers in order to reach a joint (and final) decision about a mutual matter that the several managers are jointly competent to decide upon.

☐ The authority to make a final decision with people outside the company.

☐ The authority to initiate action in areas indirectly related to the manager's assigned functions. (It has been found that delegation of such authority is especially avoided where such action could conceivably result in damage if it were to fail.) Lack of delegation of authority over peripheral areas is very common, even when the risk of failure is small (and the damage would be minor), and when successful results would clearly provide a substantial benefit to the company.

☐ The authority to develop policy and procedures in matters that are not entirely within the scope of the manager's assigned functions.

☐ The authority to arrange for experimental use of new procedures by others who are not subordinates but who work in a functional area that provides services or input to the manager.

□ The authority to make a decision and take action (when the boss, who usually does the deciding, is not available) regarding matters clearly related to the work at hand.

□ The authority to eliminate the performance of some of his own work, which the manager is convinced is unproductive and makes no contribution to the company, although procedures require him to do it.

BENEFITS RESULTING FROM
ACQUIRED AUTHORITY

As a rule, a foresighted company does not knowingly ignore or immobilize an existing profit potential. For example, it would not have a deliberate policy dictating that cash assets be kept in a safety deposit box, where they would gather dust but no income. Unused authority may be likened to unused capital, in that sense. Since authority is the power to carry out constructive action, a positive program that encourages managers to acquire dormant authority— and put it to use—prevents the loss of such profit.

Thus the two principal benefits of acquired authority is that (1) it puts a prime asset of the company to greater use, and (2) it has a favorable impact on the managerial force. Encouraging the use of acquired authority helps to solve the widespread problem of managerial dissatisfaction arising from lack of opportunity to be responsible and to exercise authority. Many companies suffer from high turnover in talented junior and middle management because of frustrations resulting from this condition. Here are some needs of managers that can be satisfied by giving these people a chance to acquire and use authority:

□ Opportunity for greater self-expression.
□ Fulfillment of a drive for more action.
□ Increased sense of contribution.
□ Enjoyment of the weight of responsibility and power.
□ Enhancement of prestige.
□ Ambition to advance.
□ Increased sense of security.
□ Personal desire to change things for the better.

☐ Opportunity to control the factors that make it possible to meet assigned responsibility.

Besides the benefits that result from retaining a satisfied group of competent managers, there is this truism to remember: Just a little more authority often enables a manager to perform at a significantly higher level.

SOME BASIC CHARACTERISTICS
OF ACQUIRED AUTHORITY

Acquired authority resembles delegated authority in some of its key features, but differs radically from it in others. An understanding of both the similarities and differences can be enlightening as to the nature and usefulness of acquired authority.

Acquired authority is similar to delegated authority in that (1) it represents power to make decisions, to take action, and to require others to follow direction and orders; (2) it can be used well or badly; (3) it can be delegated to subordinates by the man who acquired it; and (4) it can apply to a wide range of functions.

Acquired authority *differs* from delegated authority in that (1) it can be used by a subordinate without his superior's immediate awareness; (2) it must sometimes be used in a very discreet, or even clandestine, way; and (3) it is generally used with vigor (although perhaps quietly so) because a man does not usually take the initiative to acquire authority if he does not intend to use it. (Delegated authority, on the other hand, may be used hesitantly, or not at all.)

WHEN IS ACQUISITION OF
AUTHORITY UNACCEPTABLE?

From management's standpoint, there are circumstances in which it is obviously undesirable for managers to seek acquisition of authority on their own initiative. Some general yardsticks that indicate whether or not acquisition of authority is acceptable are: compatibility with company policy, the intent of the person acquiring the authority, the possibility that even the most effective use of acquired authority will not be helpful to the company in the long run, and the degree of potential damage that could result from incompetent use of acquired authority.

In a company that intends to encourage acquisition of authority, management can be helpful by defining specific situations in which there is likely to be some question as to whether or not supervisors should seek acquired authority. Here are some typical circumstances in which supervisors should be cautious in exercising their initiative to assume administrative power:

□ The authority that would be acquired is already specifically delegated to, or is at least strongly implied for use by, someone else in the organization.

□ Another manager is already actively pursuing acquisition of the same authority.

□ The authority to be acquired is not related in any way to functions or tasks assigned to the power-seeking supervisor, nor would acquisition of it be helpful in carrying out more effectively the functions or tasks that he is already performing.

□ There is a detectable degree of suspicion that the acquisition of authority may not benefit the company.

□ The acquiring supervisor is not sure that he is qualified or competent to put the authority to use.

□ There is some form of company prohibition against acquiring the authority in question.

□ The motive for acquiring authority is obviously for the individual's, rather than the company's, benefit.

Invariably, there are people in the company who can cite objections to the acquisition of practically any form or degree of authority. From the management standpoint, if the company is interested in utilizing potential authority, the list of prohibitions should be limited to conditions that would definitely be damaging. The climate for encouraging acquisition of authority is usually difficult enough to create, without establishing unnecessarily strict and sweeping impediments.

5 * HOW TO
ACQUIRE AUTHORITY

By definition, acquired authority is the power that a manager gains by his own efforts. The authority is taken, not delegated. This chapter discusses techniques for acquiring, on your own initiative, the power you may never gain by delegation and, thus, never have the opportunity to use for the company's benefit and for personal advancement. (Illustrations of these techniques in action are given in Chapter 6.)

Niccolò Machiavelli was a fifteenth century Italian statesman (that is, a politician) and a writer on matters of government. He was an all-time expert in double-dealing whose deceitful and crafty modus operandi and renown as a hypocrite were to warrant him a place in the language. (The word "Machiavellian" is used to characterize behavior or principles suggesting duplicity and cunning.)

There is no intent here of providing instructions for a would-be Machiavelli. In today's environment, the use of deceit and hypocrisy in acquiring authority are unnecessary and unwise as a means of increasing personal influence. Acquired authority should be striven for with no less good faith than that which motivates you to strive for an increase in the authority formally delegated to you. Hopefully, in both situations, the intent will be to use your administrative power for the benefit of the company. In any case, it is the intention here to suggest only methods and techniques that are morally and legally acceptable by today's standards.

This applies equally, in the chapters that follow, to managers and their superiors—that is, to all members of management.

When a manager seeks to broaden his area of influence, he should try to develop a sixth sense—a sense of perspective. A manager's self-development can be endangered by an out-of-proportion view of the significance and relevance of self-acquired authority. In this regard, it is helpful to keep two basic rules in mind: (1) The acquisition of authority is not an end in itself, and (2) the attempt to acquire authority should not be made unless you are willing to be held responsible for the judgment you used in deciding that you would acquire it.

LEARNING TO RECOGNIZE OPPORTUNITIES

The ability to recognize a set of opportunistic circumstances for acquiring authority is usually a self-developed skill. There are relatively simple means for developing an alertness to situations in which you can move to gain power that can be used favorably for you and your company. Some of these methods are explained here in detail to illustrate that the manager should have no difficulty in developing the required skill.

Try to acquire a companywide, or at least a departmentwide, view of the business. Too often, we tend to be parochial in our outlook. Our attention is limited to the immediate environment of our own job. A limited perspective of the business is bound to produce a limited understanding of the constructive things that can be done for the company. Make an effort to keep an eye on the "big picture." It provides a background against which you can identify factors that are currently important or troublesome and areas in which solutions would produce benefits, as seen from a higher level than your own. From this elevation, you have a continuing vantage point for developing ideas about the kinds of action you can take at your own level, actions that your boss will recognize as being worthwhile.

Many tools are available to help the manager maintain a high-level point of view. He can legitimately examine a wide range of key documents that will provide a continuing insight as to what is important to the company at any given time. These include both periodic and one-time reports concerning management information, operational statistics, and the findings of audits and reviews of company operations. Perusal of daily or "reading" files of significant outgoing and incoming correspondence sharpens the manager's vision of important trends and events. The agenda and minutes of high-level meetings are an invaluable source of inside information. Beyond these documented sources, he should seek permission to sit in as an occasional observer in key management meetings.

The interested supervisor should make a habit of informally discussing current events of importance with knowledgeable acquaintances throughout the company, even in casual encounters. This sort of continuing background serves to point up areas in which the ultimate acquisition of authority is easier than usual to justify, has faster payoff, and gains greater recognition for you. It also furnishes leads as to where to look for authority vacuums in or near your own area—power gaps that can be exploited for the company's benefit.

Be aware of the pattern of officially delegated authority in the company. With this knowledge, you can avoid the danger of unknowingly crossing the boundary into someone else's assigned area. In most companies, such delegations can readily be determined in organization charts, functional statements, job descriptions, and policy and procedures manuals. Whenever possible, it is a good idea, too, to get a line on implied delegations of authority, as well as authority that has been, or is in the process of being, unofficially acquired. The latter information is not always easy to gain, since it takes the form of underground intelligence, which is seldom broadcast or written about while still unofficial. Such information can best be acquired by maintaining contact with acquaintances throughout the company and by looking for clues in documented material.

There are cases on record in which managers have made a specialty of acquiring authority that had been delegated to other supervisors, either officially or semiofficially, but which was not being utilized at all by them. In this somewhat perilous technique, the manager takes advantage of the fact that the area has already been identified as being important to the company for the exercise of authority. Therefore, the incumbent of such a position cannot complain too loudly if someone else comes up with a reasonable explanation of why he has moved into that area of authority. However, this is no place for a novice to spread his wings; only highly sophisticated practitioners of the art of acquisition should apply their skills in such an area.

Analyze continuing or recurring problems, failures, lack of accomplishment, and other symptoms of troubled performance in the company or department. An attempt should be made, through observation and discussion with others, to trace these symptoms back to their origins. Look particularly for basic ills or unsatisfactory conditions in areas that are within the grasp of your initiative (connected somehow with your functional responsibilities). Determine if the unsatisfactory situation is the result of unused opportunities to apply authority. The use of acquired authority to correct an unsatisfactory condition is often the easiest and most acceptable exercise of such authority.

Put your imagination to work. In doing so, the imagination should be focused or directed in a way that will stimulate it to be productive. Seek out a quiet atmosphere for several hours, somewhere away from the daily working atmosphere, if possible. Construct in your mind a mental model of the unit or department in which you work—a kind of semidetailed mental picture or diagram of how the component operates, what it does, and the functions, systems, and tasks within it. The degree of detail need not be extensive for the model to be useful. With such a model in mind (and being as truthful and objective about it as possible), imagine that it is your business, that you own or operate it as you see fit. Speculate as to what kinds of actions or undertakings you would perform in operating the business. Jot down brief descriptions of the things you imagine you would do. Then review the list of ideas and analyze them from a very practical and realistic standpoint. This technique often provides clues to areas in which you can profitably acquire authority and accomplish worthwhile objectives, even if you don't own the company.

Develop a continuing and broad knowledge of new and emerging techniques, methods, and processes that are potentially applicable in your company. Keep in touch with the ideas being developed and applied elsewhere in the industry, or in business in general. Awareness of new concepts may help you visualize or recognize how they can be used in areas in which you might have an opportunity to expand your responsibility and authority.

There are many tools available for sharpening the ability to recognize opportunities for acquiring authority. Those described above will suggest others. The point is, the manager can prepare himself by developing a broadened vision of his opportunities, and thus be ready to detect situations in which he can increase his contribution to the company by applying the potential but unused authority that exists in most companies.

THE RULES ARE FLEXIBLE

Most of us receive our management training in an atmosphere and a format that tend to indicate that the manager must act within certain prescribed limits in order to be successful. As a result, the typical supervisor manages "by the book" until he acquires enough knowledge and wisdom to understand that a flexible approach to management is much more realistic and profitable. This evolution toward a more liberal attitude concerning the rules ultimately reaches our most deeply entrenched beliefs—those pertaining to the very basic functions of management, such as the exercise of authority. It seems that our teachers, in school and in the business world, indoctrinated us most rigidly in the fundamental tenets of management.

Supervisors who maintain a doctrinaire approach to management tend to view delegated authority as a magic wand, as though the very act of delegation provides the possessor with all the wit he needs to exercise the authority in a useful way. In fact, many managers do not understand that the possession of authority is not, in itself, the essential factor that enables them to wield important power. Rather, it is the combination of the supervisor's delegated authority (which is relatively limited) and the fact that he is responsible for almost everything within his purview. It is up to him to use his authority, his initiative, his ingenuity, and his ambition to get the job done within acceptable bounds of conduct. Successful performance by an enterprise or by an individual manager does not depend so much on the exact configuration of delegated authority as on an understanding of how responsibility can amplify authority. Profitable performance is the result of knowing when to bring authority into play in a given situation, and how to apply power so as to achieve beneficial trade-offs among the various options that exist in the contest. For the individual manager, the optimum pattern of authority is based more on a sense of involvement in company affairs (that is, a sense of responsibility) than on dependence on the "license" that spells out his delegated authority. Keeping this in mind, we should not be surprised to find in the real world of business that there are often successful exceptions to such long-standing and deeply cherished principles of authority as:

☐ A manager should take orders from only one man.
☐ A manager doesn't do the work himself, but exercises his authority through others.
☐ A manager devotes most of his time to supervising subordinates.
☐ A manager must have authority that is equal to his responsibility.

These are some of the traditional rules we are taught to hold inviolate until experience teaches us that they are not sacred. In contrast, here are some of the facts of managerial life that are often more important than the rules in determining how a manager receives and applies his authority.

☐ A small percentage of a manager's time is spent with his subordinates.
☐ Concepts such as authority, power, and responsibility—

though very much in practice—are rarely discussed. "Talking about it" does little good as a way of solving problems and getting the job done.

□ There is a paramount need to develop relationships with a range and variety of people in preparation for future situations and the circumstances peculiar to them. These relationships are likely to be tested during the course of difficult negotiations.

□ Skill in administrative arts and in dealing with people is much more useful than technical sophistication in the proficient application of authority.

□ Fast footwork in making decisions and in applying authority is usually a more dominant factor than the exact shade and degree of authority that has been delegated.

Even if we accept the reality that the textbook rules of authority in management are usually changeable, the fact remains that some managers do work in companies or departments having rigid patterns of delegated authority. There are entire industries that, by their very nature, have a strong tendency toward a fixed, authoritarian structure. The supervisor confronted with such an impediment to his desire for acquiring authority undoubtedly has a difficult problem. However, there is a positive way to look at this kind of situation: In such companies, the potential authority lying about waiting to be picked up is simply tremendous. Thus it is all the more worthwhile for the ambitious man to move (with discretion) in the direction of acquiring authority. It is a matter of picking the right time, place, and boss before making the move—and then proceeding cautiously. To say the least, top management in companies suffering from such rigidity would be surprised if they were to objectively examine the benefits that could accrue if the strings of authority were loosened a little.

TAKING A CHANCE ON POWER

In fairness, it must be said that the man who seeks to acquire more authority always runs the risk of encountering penalties and reprisals. In many companies and situations, he may be strongly rebuffed if he proceeds to use his initiative in a direct and straightforward way. He takes a chance on losing ground while attempting to move ahead, with the possibility of being embarrassed and ridiculed. Therefore, it is often necessary to be very cautious and indirect, to feel one's way along, and to pick the most opportune situation to acquire a little bit of responsibility and authority. The manager is rarely shut out completely from gaining ground. Even in a landscape where obstacles exist in profusion in the path of the independently minded supervisor, it is worth his time and effort to use a little initiative and risk a small reprisal.

There is an interesting phenomenon that can be useful to the manager seeking to gain leverage from the flexibility in the rules, a way of diminishing the risks of being rebuffed when trying to gain power. It is this: The acquisition of authority can often follow (rather than precede) the assumption of responsibility. It is very tempting, especially to the uninitiated, to aim directly for the authority, since immediate acquisition of it appears to be more advantageous and beneficial than assumption of responsibility. Frequently, however, and for many reasons, responsibility should be sought out first. Some managers discover a greater degree of satisfaction in going this route, particularly since the assumption of responsibility can be a tangible sign of achievement and prestige. Of even more significance to all managers, other persons in the organization, who might object quickly if you are seen reaching for authority, are much less concerned if you appear to be picking up the burden of responsibility.

A LOW-RISK APPROACH

The most elementary method of acquiring authority, which is also the lowest risk method for both company and manager, is the "creeping responsibility" technique. This means moving out gradually, in a way virtually unnoticed by others. The technique is also compatible with the principle stated earlier that it is tactically sounder to move out and encompass responsibility first and, subsequently, the authority that goes with it. This method is applicable and useful, regardless of whether the general climate regarding authority in the company is permissive or conservative.

In addition to the premise that the assuming of responsibility for a given area enhances the opportunity for acquiring authority, there is another useful and valid principle: The manager should seek responsibility (and then authority) in those regions that interface with the operational and functional areas where he is already using authority in a highly visible and emphatic manner. The scope of his existing authority is thereby increased by gradually spreading out from his existing power base to adjacent areas.

This concept of "gradually spreading out" takes advantage of an almost universal characteristic of the modern organization structure. Officially delegated and implied areas of authority actually resemble small islands of power scattered across the huge and largely unoccupied landscape of total potential authority in the company. Such topography presents endless opportunities to advance quietly outside your base without attracting sudden attention.

In this analogy, the islands represent authority actually assigned and in use. The wide open spaces between each area of defined authority represent the gray areas in which potential authority exists and is up for acquisition. Since we have this reality of a power structure with "holes" in it, the prime technique for acquiring authority—in either an opportunistic or a premeditated way—is to explore the gray areas in the structure, beginning with those that surround your own island of defined authority.

Here are some of the mechanics for moving into the nearby gray areas of potential authority.

Always be sure that you are moving into a reasonably safe area, in which no one else already possesses delegated or implied authority. Be sure, too, that you are willing and able to accept the responsibility that goes with the use of acquired authority. In fact, wherever feasible, demonstrate your responsibility first, and your authority second. For example, if you find that higher management has a question or problem pertaining to something closely related to your assigned area of authority, but in a gray area outside of it, assume the responsibility for answering the question or problem. It could be a first step in acquiring the parallel authority.

Acquire authority for some useful purpose. It is seldom meaningful for you to move in and take over authority on speculation, with the hope that something may happen that will permit you to put the authority to use. Before seeking to acquire the authority, establish first that you can do something constructive with it. Do not stake a claim unless you are reasonably sure there is pay dirt around. If you cannot put the authority to good use, it may become an embarrassing burden, for someone may ask to see your results. Action, even if it is cautious and obscured, should follow closely upon your first move to acquire authority.

Acquired authority must be handled and used more sensitively and carefully than delegated authority. Delegated authority is, in itself, your license to take action and there is seldom any need to explain why you are using it. In contrast, acquired authority frequently must be used at first (even if only for a very short period) in a guarded, subtle, and perhaps even covert fashion. It is not that there is anything wrong in using authority that has been conscientiously acquired, but mainly it is to avoid the possibility of questions or conflicts about your right to use it before you have had a chance to show results. Premature disclosure may raise disagreements as to who should have the authority, whether or not it exists at all, and how it should be used. Early conflict of this kind can be embarrassing and may stifle the emergence of potential authority in the embattled area for a long time.

Acquired authority should be brought along gently, but not necessarily slowly. It is important that each succeeding use of the authority be added in a logical way to a well-built base constructed from the previous use of the authority. When it finally emerges and becomes clearly visible to others, it carries with it a history of successive use and successful results.

When management first becomes officially aware that you are operating in an area of acquired authority, it should be made to recognize instantly that you not only hold yourself responsible for proper use of such authority, but that you have produced benefits to the company by using it. Obviously, this is an objective (rather than an absolutely mandatory condition), since you cannot always avoid management's awareness of your actions before you are ready to make them known. However, if your actions are planned toward this objective, even if you are discovered prematurely, your accomplishments thus far at least provide evidence of your sincerity and responsibility. In cases where you have been able to maintain control of the situation and are ready to make your acquired authority known to management, do it in such a way that the results, and your acceptance of responsibility for the situation, are highly evident.

PRINCIPLES OF ADVANCED ACQUISITION
OF AUTHORITY

Although the "creeping responsibility" approach to acquisition of authority is a primary and important tool for the interested manager, there are more sophisticated techniques for the experienced practitioner. First, we consider eight *principles* of advanced acquisition (and look at some of the techniques later):

(1) A good way to expand your authority is to develop, intensively and extensively, the power that you already have. Don't waste your time in new territories until you have fully exploited the area of power that unquestionably belongs to you now.

(2) The best kind of authority to acquire is the kind you can use to make a contribution to the company. It will last longer and get you further than any authority you acquire for purely personal benefit.

(3) You can't expect, on the basis of one or two instances of use of acquired authority, to establish a permanent claim to it. Unless you apply it consistently, and use some acceptable method to secure official recognition of the authority, you may have to establish over and over again your right to employ it.

(4) When you have used your acquired authority diligently, try to provide your boss with some easy way to acknowledge that you have a legitimate claim to the power

and that it is within the scope of authority inherent in his position. This adds considerable strength to your hold on the authority. (Naturally, if he disclaims that it is within his province to do so, you are likely to have trouble holding on to the acquired authority.)

(5) As a general rule, avoid jurisdictional battle with anyone who can show that the authority in question is officially delegated to him, even though he may not have used it. Back off and attempt to redefine the authority you wish to acquire, in such a way that it does not conflict with the official delegation. At the same time, do what you can to encourage the other manager to put his authority to use constructively. If he fails, it may serve to convince him that he shouldn't make an issue of your attempts to apply the authority.

(6) A good source for finding out what authority you can seek to acquire (so that you can do your job better) is any document that officially states what authority is delegated in the areas in which you are interested. Analysis of such documents may reveal the exact direction in which you should proceed.

(7) Suppose you want very much to acquire and use authority in a certain area. If you cannot determine whether or not someone already has such authority, use it just once yourself—in a tentative way—and see if anyone reacts strongly.

(8) If you desire to use the authority that you know is not assigned to anyone, act as though it is really yours to use. On almost every occasion, others will accept your use of it and not question your right to apply it.

ADVANCED TECHNIQUES FOR
ACQUIRING AUTHORITY

With an understanding of the principles that apply to the more sophisticated ways of acquiring authority, we are now in a position to examine the means themselves—some techniques for use by the experienced acquirer. There are many, and the ones described here (which can be used separately or in combination) will suggest others. Again, it should be remembered that it is not to the manager's advantage, or to the benefit of the company, to practice deceit or to act in a hypocritical way in acquiring authority. It usually makes sense to govern our actions by a sense of commitment to the company and its best interests. We should exercise discretion and judgment so as not to exceed the accepted bounds of morality.

Exerting Pressure on Others
A very useful form of acquiring authority is to exert pressure on others in the company to carry out actions in their areas of responsibility so that you can do your particular job better. This method of expanding your authority is very practical, and is justifiable on the basis that it is directly related to increasing your contribution to the company. It is a good starting point for gaining expertise in acquiring authority on your own initiative. Its unsatisfactory side-effects are usually limited, even in a company with a very conservative approach. Basically, you are endeavoring to get someone else to do his job so that you can do yours. The authority thus acquired is really only a step or two beyond a kind of implied authority that is present in most positions. The implication is that you are entitled to execute unspecified actions in order to carry out your job responsibilities.

For example, this kind of authority would pertain in the case of a supervisory buyer who asks an engineering supervisor to develop expanded technical data so that the buyers can solicit additional suppliers in order to get a better price. Another example is the sales manager who pressures the production scheduling unit to look for ways of meeting a short delivery date. If it could be accomplished, it would open the way for a large order from an anxious customer. To make the proposition more acceptable, the buying supervisor could indicate his willingness to ask the assistant superintendent of production for overtime for the job.

When you demand or convince someone else to maximize his efforts to take action, you have carried out the primary step in the process of acquiring authority. In a way, you are acting like a boss in ordering or persuading the other man to carry out his responsibilities. However, it is important to bear in mind the fact that indiscriminate use of this kind of acquired authority can make enemies and arouse effective resistance. Elementary as this form of acquired authority is, the application of it requires a certain style and tempo. There is usually someone in the organization who is bound to react strongly to almost any attempt to acquire authority in or near his functional area. Such an individual visualizes this action as upsetting the balance of power and possibly endangering his position. Be alert to the possibility that any kind of acquisition of authority may require a degree of finesse and subtlety to counteract a possible unfavorable reaction.

"Phasing In" Your Authority

Another relatively safe method for acquiring authority is via an action that enables you to operate almost entirely within the framework of a function presently delegated to you. For example, suppose you discover a better way of carrying out a responsibility, a method that departs from previous practice. In using it, you may drift somewhat outside your zone of delegated authority. Therefore, it becomes necessary to acquire authority in order to fully carry out your concept.

Consider the case of a supervisor in need of three additional workers. Normally, he depends on the personnel department to do the hiring for his unit. He happens to know there are some good candidates available in a nearby city, because they work for a company that is laying off employees at a rapid rate. To be sure that a prompt invitation is extended to these people to apply for work in his company, the supervisor makes direct contact with a mutual acquaintance and asks him to tell the men to apply quickly to his personnel department. Although, by this action, he is assuming the authority to do some personnel recruiting, he sees to it that they go to the personnel department for employment interviews. Thus, while remaining reasonably close to the procedure, the supervisor has taken the initiative to put into effect a beneficial change, involving activity that is marginal in terms of the scope of his formal authority. In this way, he has acquired and used some power, which should not be offensive to the personnel department because they still exercise their fundamental authority to officially hire new employees.

This type of acquired authority permits you to take a step outside your delegated area by using it as a power base toward which you can withdraw if necessary. In a way, it is "phased" authority in that if the first phase is successful, you can continue to broaden it to other, bolder steps of acquiring authority.

Preparing Details for Your Action

One particular method of acquiring authority is characterized by detailed preparation for your action. Its basic intent is to enable you to make or influence decisions, actually outside your delegated scope of authority, by means of a confrontation. You have been aware on many occasions, for instance, that a decision is going to be made on the basis of information to be presented to an official in the company. Assume, for our purposes, you anticipate that the decision will be to follow a course of action that is less desirable for the company than the one you could sponsor or suggest. You therefore prepare yourself in detail on the subject matter of the situation. You develop the necessary facts and figures, and even practice how to make your pitch. The moment of confrontation takes place at a decision-making meeting, which you have perhaps arranged, or to which you have secured an invitation. You speak up at the appropriate time and make your prepared presentation, although it may appear to be extemporaneous.

This technique has somewhat heavier risks than others, and may attract enemies or criticism if used unwisely. However, many opportunities arise in which this approach can be used. Often, it presents an avenue for being helpful to the company by giving officials a chance to choose from a spectrum of options not otherwise available.

The authority acquired by this approach initially takes the form of a sudden, successful move to gain a strong voice in shaping a decision outside your immediate area of authority. It can be a very temporary kind of authority, which nevertheless elevates your stature because of the significance attached to the acceptance of your proposal. As a further tactic, you may be able to consolidate your position to a more permanent status by proposing a plan of action that puts you firmly into the picture with a role in implementing the decision. Or, by repeatedly coming up with well-prepared suggestions over a longer period of time, you may build a base whereby your advice is invited or sought on a regular basis.

An example of the latter method occurred in the case of a supervisor of a systems analysis group. As a member of a committee that reviewed and approved proposed computer applications, he used his membership as a means for promoting an idea that he felt would be extremely beneficial to the company. His idea—which he persistently injected into each meeting of the committee—was to build into various computer applications a technique for monitoring the future performance of the approved computer systems. His arguments for this approach were always carefully prepared for each new computer application, in the hope that he would be able to influence the majority of the committee in its favor. As a result of his continuing influence on a majority of the members, the committee ultimately recommended to management that this man's systems group be charged with the responsibility for carrying out the actual monitoring of the operation of all major ADPM systems.

Gaining the Support of Your Peers
Not only can you acquire authority by influencing your principals or other decision makers, but you can also acquire it by influencing other people on your own level. The basic tactic here is to gain the support and cooperation of your peers in accomplishing some activity that might meet with resistance if you were to seek the authority and approval through conventional channels. Assume that you have an idea for a course of action that involves your operations as well as those in other departments. You have reason to believe your principals would be reluctant to approve the idea if you presented it to them as an untried proposal. Therefore, you seek to convince them by aligning the support of

others who would be involved at your own level of operation.

A supervisor, for example, has an idea for solving a perennial problem, one which higher management has not seen fit to act on in a positive way. It has to do with a system in which he and other departments are involved. He arranges to get together informally with the other supervisors who, stimulated by this man's idea, agree on a joint course of action.They try it out on a pilot basis, in parallel with the existing system, and the results are successful. The supervisor who generated the plan then presents the results of the jointly sponsored pilot operation to higher authority as the basis for seeking approval of the revised system.

Dealing With Outsiders

A technique somewhat parallel to the above involves dealing with persons outside the company. A supervisor who, in the course of his business operations, has contact with suppliers or customers can look to this arena as a means of increasing his administrative power. Within the scope of his delegated authority, there are probably many transactions he can decide on for himself in doing business with such sources. But there are bound to be other matters outside the zone of delegated authority for making agreements.

Circumstances may arise—in connection with an area where a manager does not have delegated authority to act —in which he is virtually certain of what his boss's decision would be. On such occasion, especially when the circumstances foretell special benefit to the company if an agreement is concluded, the manager may decide to make at least a tentative commitment with an outsider on behalf of his company. He can then present it to his boss for final approval, making it clear, of course, that he has already made a provisional commitment.

Supervisors in departments such as sales, purchasing, and new business functions have special opportunities to use this technique. Agreements on various conditions of sale or purchase offer fruitful grounds for exploring ways to expand one's authority through acquisition.

Changing Your Group's Operational Techniques

Turning to internal administrative matters, there is a wide range of opportunities for expanding power via changes in procedures and operational techniques. By this means, authority can be gained on a relatively permanent basis, often with a substantial favorable impact. For example, many supervisors have considerable latitude with regard to altering the shape and character of the work outputs produced by their groups. In such an environment, the supervisor can make moves to expand and consolidate his authority in a climate of relative calm.

Consider the manager who heads a group that produces design information, drawings, and the like for a manufacturing department. He has decided that the traditional company format he has been using for such documents does not fully utilize the talent and knowledge of his group and, furthermore, causes him to follow certain inefficient practices. He has an idea for a change that not only would correct these deficiencies, but would benefit the manufacturing department receiving his output. He makes the change on his own initiative.

When the first new outputs are ready, he personally takes them to the head of that manufacturing department. He explains the change to him, emphasizing the benefits to that department. (If the design manager had previously determined that the possibility of rejection or resentment was too great to risk, he could cut the risk by carrying out the change in parallel with the old method. Thus if he meets with reluctance to accept the new format, he could present the old format as well, leaving both of them with the manufacturing department for its consideration.)

Changing Other Groups' Operational Techniques

The reverse of the above technique also offers opportunities for acquiring authority. The inputs you receive from another department afford you an opportunity to influence the operations of that group to the company's benefit. You are certainly in a position to know if a change in input would benefit your group. You also probably know enough about the operations of the producing department to evaluate whether or not a certain change will be helpful to them.

As an example of this technique, assume that you receive certain financial reports about customers from another department. These reports are not as complete or as well organized as they could be for your needs. Determine some feasible changes that would improve their usefulness to you and would pose no problems for the preparing group (or might even be beneficial to it). Then carefully select a supervisor in that group who is involved with the reports and whom you have evaluated as being potentially receptive to the idea, and visit him in his office.

In this sort of situation, it is best not to make a direct proposal concerning the change you have in mind. Rather, begin with a discussion of your own needs and problems; wonder aloud about the possible benefits of some features of your proposal (without identifying it as such). If you are skillful enough in your techniques for seeding ideas, and if the other supervisor is alert and receptive, he may pick up your thought and expand on it so that it becomes his idea. Help him reach a decision to try the new format, and offer your aid. As soon as you receive the first examples of the new output, make a point of quickly getting back to your collaborator. Praise the change as a significant improvement which he has developed. Emphasize the benefits of it to his department and encourage him to break the good news to his boss, so that he will get credit for it.

This technique provides a good illustration of an initial acquisition of authority in a given area, which can then be consolidated and expanded. Having once achieved a successful result in influencing another department, you can take advantage of your new entrée and "suggest" other ideas that will affect its operations beneficially.

This method of expanding your influence from a solid initial base is applicable to virtually every technique of acquiring authority discussed in this book. Such opportunities should never be overlooked, even in the rush to move into virgin territory. Always make the effort to consolidate and expand your successes, since the initial good results may lead to bigger ones. And do not be overly concerned about gaining immediate credit from your boss for the successes you have been instrumental in achieving. Your role in the improvements will inevitably be recognized. Even if there is a delay in recognition, it may be to your benefit, for it will come later at a time when solid achievements have been registered.

Using the Slow-and-Easy Method

The slow-and-easy method of acquiring authority is a technique that requires patience, but has a relatively low risk factor. It is particularly useful in circumstances where a speedy move toward controlling the situation would create a strong reaction, but a deliberate pace would not upset anyone.

Imagine a situation in which a first-line supervisor wants to effect a change in his operations. The modification in procedures will impact on other areas in the department, areas not under his delegated authority. Specifically, the supervisor wants to discontinue providing a certain work product to another section, which he is convinced should not be using the product at all and, in actual practice, is using it in a limited fashion. He fears that a sudden stop in forwarding the product would engender a strong reaction, since the recipient could probably point to at least some minimal use for it. So the supervisor slowly withdraws the product over a substantial period of time, by gradually lengthening the interval between deliveries and by reducing the scope and size of the product. He finds that his action evokes little or no reaction, because it is so gradual and because he was right in his evaluation that the product was of marginal use. Eventually, the issue fades and is forgotten. He has made his point and is now in a position to move to other related actions at a faster tempo because of it. His slow steps in exercising the power to make this change have opened the door for him.

Pairing Off with Another Area

Every manager is aware of certain tasks or programs that are not being performed but should be, for the benefit of the company. Perhaps you, as a manager, could successfully carry out these actions in your own group. The reason you are not performing them is that you have not been specifically authorized to do so. This kind of situation offers an exciting opportunity to expand your authority beyond the officially defined scope of your position.

A very successful technique that can be helpful in these circumstances is the one sometimes referred to as the *pairing* technique. If you decide to expand your operations into a zone currently not being exploited, pair off this area with some task you are currently doing, which you feel is of doubtful or marginal benefit to the company. The resources and attention devoted to the latter can be slowly shifted to the new area of interest, as you gradually decrease activity in the marginal task.

This technique has a special appeal in that a questionable operation is replaced by an obviously more useful one, and the necessary financing is furnished by dropping the unprofitable task. If there is a serious complaint about the reduction of operations in the area being abandoned, you can readily justify it by pointing to the area being built up. And the reverse is true, in that you may justify the buildup by explaining the declining operation.

Piloting an Operation

A variation of the above technique is the straightforward *pilot* approach. Suppose you find yourself thinking about a certain kind of customer service—a potentially profitable activity—in which your company is not currently engaged. Suppose further that, if the program were to be carried out as the result of an official decision, it could conceivably fall within your area of responsibility, if only indirectly. You therefore proceed on your own and cautiously provide the service on a limited basis, being prepared to defend your action (if it is challenged) on the grounds that it is a test, or pilot, operation. If a rationale is needed for not seeking prior approval, it could be based on the fact that you didn't want to bother management with the idea until you had tested it.

Once you are committed to a pilot operation, support it

strongly with the resources available to you. As a method of extra protection against possible criticism, it is sometimes feasible to approach a sympathetic executive who is not your boss. Explain your idea, but do not ask for his approval or aid. If he indicates that he thinks it is a good idea, this may be helpful to you later.

If the pilot operation produces good results in the initial run, keep it going long enough to secure documented evidence of success. Then create an opportunity to present the idea to your principals, as high up the chain as possible (being careful to bring the intermediate supervisors into the picture in advance, or at the same time). Present the idea initially as a proposal, and demonstrate your knowledge and proficiency in that area. At the strategic moment, reveal the successful results of your pilot operation.

THE SIGNIFICANCE OF INITIATIVE
IN ACQUIRING AUTHORITY

The practical techniques and methods of acquiring authority that are described above are illustrative only. They in no way represent a complete list of possible approaches to gaining power. Nevertheless, even this sampling serves to make a significant point about the role of personal initiative in expanding one's power and influence in an organization.

Initiative is almost always the starting point in the campaign to acquire authority. It is the first essential ingredient. Yet we sometimes find managers who have neither the will nor the incentive to act on their own initiative without being urged or directed. They are reluctant to deliberately and voluntarily take on the responsibility for the kind of action that leads to acquisition of authority. Initiative and acquisition of power naturally go together. By definition, acquired authority is the power that a man seeks out and takes of his own volition, without being directed to do so by his bosses. Thus he obviously *takes the initiative* to acquire authority. Without initiative, the process of expanding one's power can never begin.

The feat of acquiring authority is really an act of creativity. In the process, the manager first perceives dimly, then more definitely, the activity he can make happen, activity that will be beneficial to the company. This vision often produces an understanding that the "something" that can be accomplished is not really within anyone's assigned functions. Therefore, nothing will happen unless the manager who recognizes the shortcoming takes the necessary steps to get the process moving. Hopefully, the manager is motivated by a drive to accomplish the objectives he perceives and a willingness to accept responsibility for implementing a creative course of action. The man who seeks to use his initiative must be willing not only to be responsible for putting his creative ideas into effect, but to live with the results.

The manager who uses his initiative to get things done via the route of acquired authority often may have to engage in a frontal attack against the notion that he can only be effective by moving up, over, and down through the formal network of the organization. The unfortunate truth is that for many kinds of necessary activity, these channels are often clogged with slow-moving traffic. Along this path, the manager is likely to encounter some degree of disinterest concerning the matters he is interested in; that is, activities such as the unspectacular exchange of information and influence that are absolutely necessary in order for the organization to operate in a coordinated fashion. The successful foreman, supervisor, or middle-level executive knows when to avoid formal channels and make his contacts directly across the organization. Of course, he also recognizes those occasions on which it is mandatory or advantageous to use the organization's formal lines. He influences people on many levels to do what they can or should do, so that he can accomplish what he perceives as necessary to the welfare of the company.

A manager in this position must believe that he has not only the responsibility to tell others what he expects of them, but also the authority to enforce his belief. He must extend his initiative to the point where he assumes the authority to cajole, convince, or even demand others to do what must be done for the good of the company.

Obviously, there are risks involved for the manager who

exercises his initiative. He may be rebuffed, penalized, or even suffer reprisals on occasion. He may have to take two steps backward before he can move one step forward. To minimize these risks, he must use discretion and good judgment, and sometimes move cautiously and indirectly, so as not to exceed reasonable bounds in his insistence on action. The surest guide to reasonable action in using initiative is a lively sense of commitment to the interests of the company. This is the essence of management: the true desire to become involved in the affairs of your company and the resultant motivation to use initiative to jump into the mainstream of activity. Every manager is invited into the channels of company activity, but only to a point. From there on in, it is up to the manager—and his initiative—to determine whether or not he stays in the mainstream, and how far into it he moves.

A personal involvement in the affairs of the company makes the supervisor feel accountable for the things he does, as well as for things he does not do. (He should know that he is wrong, for example, if he takes no action on a problem of which he is aware, but others are not.) This sense of involvement focuses his interest on those factors in the business that are important to top management. Thus he acquires the habits and attitudes of a responsible manager, a man who measures his actions in terms of the good of the company. He exercises his initiative out of a sense of responsibility as a member of company management, and not solely as a supervisor of one section of the company. Obviously, this approach to management greatly broadens the area in which the manager feels he can and should take constructive action.

6 * EXAMPLES OF ACQUIRING AUTHORITY

This chapter presents a series of examples in which individual supervisors and executives go about the process of acquiring authority. All these managers have real-life counterparts. The reader may recognize a similarity to business people he has known and perhaps wondered about concerning their rise to power. The cases are presented in various formats to suit the circumstances and to illustrate that authority can be acquired in many different ways and situations.

A CASE OF QUIET BUT STEADY ACQUISITION

To forestall the assumption that acquisition of authority always involves a dramatic incident, we consider first a typical routine case of expanding the power base. It serves to demonstrate that a significant degree and type of authority can be acquired and accumulated in a calm and workaday manner within the daily context of the job. This is the way the professional often operates, when circumstances permit. Dramatic confrontations and loud competition for power are usually reserved for effect, or as a last resort. The individual authority-gathering actions of the central figure in this case may seem to be mundane and of relatively little impact. But it should be remembered that the acquisition of small increments of power on a continuing basis soon amounts to a significant increase in real authority in the organization.

This is the case of Frank McHugh, who has successfully acquired authority in a series of small packages. Consequently, he has made a considerable contribution to the well-being of his company and has been handsomely recognized for it. McHugh is the assistant superintendent in an assembly department of a medium-size manufacturing company that specializes in metal household furnishings. The success of his department not only depends on the productivity of its members and their individual skills, but leans heavily on the cooperation and performance of many other groups within the company, as well as some people outside the company.

McHugh has a competent and interested group of supervisors, foremen, and senior employees working for him. He is quite satisfied that they can effectively carry out 90 percent of the department's work, with only general guidance from him. The other 10 percent represents special situations, which command more of his attention, yet account for not quite half his working hours. It is interesting to note that the authority officially delegated to McHugh, as well as the authority clearly implied in his position, is almost entirely related to internal operations in his department. However, he believes that the difference between adequate performance and superior accomplishment by his group depends on the extent to which he can achieve cooperation and action from a great variety of people outside his department.

McHugh, then, spends about half his time in his shop and the other half with people other than his direct subordinates. Some (though not very much) of his time outside the shop is spent with his immediate boss and other higher executives. He is content to let his boss—the department head—take care of policy matters through the more official channels of the organization. McHugh, therefore, expends a very substantial portion of his working hours dealing with a great variety of people within, and some outside, the company on an informal and unstructured basis. He is highly motivated to put his initiative to work via the informal organization, both horizontally and diagonally, convincing people to do things so that his department can do its job better.

When we consider the magnitude of the interfaces between any key department in a company and all the other departments it is involved with, it is easy to visualize how extensive and numerous the potential contacts are that can be made at various levels in the organization. A manufacturing department has a wide range of interrelationships with other groups in the company, from accounting at one end to warehousing at the other, plus all stops between. In each related group, there is something that can be done—or not done—to facilitate the work of a manufacturing department.

If we follow McHugh for several hours to observe his initiative at work, we see some examples of acquired authority in operation, such as these:

(1) McHugh visits with the head of the design unit in the engineering services department to discuss the redesign of a shelf unit. The unit is a high-volume sales item for the company, but it poses certain assembly problems that add to its cost. The two men have discussed this subject before, and McHugh now urges the designer to start the project quickly. Together, they go to the designer's boss, the assistant head of the department. McHugh relates from memory the cost, sales, and profit figures on a number of items that require engineering service, but have priority over his project. Graphically portraying the benefits to be derived from redesign of the shelf unit, he convinces the two engineers that his own project is more important in terms of company profit. He helps them rearrange the priorities of the various projects, managing to place his own pet project at the top of the list.

(2) McHugh then descends a flight of stairs to the personnel office to talk to the head of the employment unit about recruiting two machine operators, an action his department has just requested. He cites two special requirements that he would like the employment unit to look for in candidates for these jobs. The employment supervisor indicates that these qualifications are not within the normal requirements of the job description used by recruiters to evaluate candidates for such jobs. McHugh states that it will be a waste of time to send him people who do not meet these special requirements, since he simply will not consider them for the jobs. Although he is firm about his feelings in

the matter, he is not offensive, and eases out of the conversation with two of his favorite jokes.

(3) McHugh returns to his office for a few minutes, then leaves the company property to keep a luncheon engagement with an executive of a firm that supplies large quantities of washers, shims, locknuts, and similar items to the company. These items are important in the assembly operation carried out by his department. He explains a problem being encountered in the use of certain special washers (samples of which he has brought along), and asks the supplier to correct it by changing the metallic content and finish. Because an increase in price is involved, he agrees to accept a change in the quantity specified for delivery in the current contract. For the total price agreed to in the contract, McHugh states he will accept a 15 percent decrease in quantity if the supplier changes the item specifications. He also pays for the lunch.

This example of how an initiative-oriented executive operates and how he acquires and uses power within reasonable bounds illustrates the mechanics of expansion of authority. In (1), McHugh assumed the authority to reshape the priority of the engineering projects requested by the manufacturing department. Normally, this authority is exercised by an executive who is two levels higher than McHugh in the organization. The latter feels justified in using the authority in this case because he is familiar with the circumstances of all the projects involved. He is reassured, too, by the fact that his reasoning about the order of priorities stood up in the face of severe questioning by the engineering officials. (He made a mental note to present an after-the-fact justification of this rearrangement to his boss and to the executive who normally makes such decisions.)

In (2), McHugh was exceeding the normal limits of the agreement between his department and the personnel office regarding the standard requirements in hiring people for certain types of jobs. He is actually in a position in which he can reject candidates sent to him by the personnel people. (Of course, he is expected to have very good reasons for doing so; otherwise, he would be challenged by the recruiters.) Therefore, he is simply being demanding and critical *before* the fact, by adding new requirements in advance. This action may contradict the letter of agreement between his boss and the personnel department, but it does not violate the spirit of the agreement. So it is a special case. McHugh justifies his action as an early and effective use of authority that he would normally use later on anyway, and perhaps with less desirable results.

In (3), McHugh is admittedly expanding his authority in a consequential way into the area of the purchasing department. He has negotiated a change in the specifications, quantity, and price features of an official, executed contract. But it should be noted that he probably would have had little difficulty in getting these requirements included in the contract originally, had he been sure of them at the time. Also, his department has the general authority to inspect and accept deliveries of material contracted for it. Within this authority, there is a certain amount of practical leeway and flexibility in the process of accepting material. As far as McHugh is concerned, it is a short step from exercising this delegated authority to making an agreement to change the conditions of acceptance of material prior to performance on the contract.

A SUPERVISOR TAKES A CHANCE
—AND SUCCEEDS

An electric utility company serving the suburban area of a large midwestern city had an increasing volume of sales each year. It was a gradual increase and the company profited from it, especially because it did not require any extraordinary investments in capital equipment or construction to support the increased volume. The reason for this was that the plant had been designed for a far greater capacity than was originally needed to satisfy the company's own customers. The company, therefore, had been selling a large volume of its excess electrical power to the large utility corporation that serviced urban customers in the nearby city. Sales to that utility customer were made at low prices, which covered direct costs plus only a portion of related overhead costs.

Connie Wallace, a senior sales representative and supervisor in the sales promotion department, was pleased with this evidence of company progress, though she sometimes wondered if the company might be actually falling behind rather than moving ahead. Her reasoning was that the rising sales volume was not keeping pace with the rate of increasing population in the suburban area covered by her company. She felt that the company was not getting its share of new business. In terms of percentages, it appeared to be losing ground in the competitive race with other fuels.

Miss Wallace analyzed the pattern of population growth and dwelling construction. She came to the conclusion that the company, in fact, was making a sufficient effort to encourage builders and developers of private housing units to install electric stoves, cooling and heating units, and other electric appliances and equipment. But for all other construction—apartment houses, motor inns, office buildings, and institutions—the company had an entirely inadequate promotion program, and made little direct effort to capture the market. She reasoned that it would be worthwhile to make a strong attempt to influence key design and construction people connected with these types of buildings, because one sale would result in a massive commitment to electric power.

Miss Wallace felt convinced that she should personally attempt to do something about this potentially profitable market for her company. Normally, she was authorized to spend funds on various budgeted promotion activities, and she had an entertainment allowance as well. Although there were no specific limitations as to the kinds of builders she could contact and entertain, it was generally taken for granted—and vaguely understood—that the market consisted of builders of private homes.

She began her campaign by studying publications that pertained to construction other than private dwellings, using funds allocated to her group to secure such publications. She consulted various acquaintances in these sectors of construction, and also used her group's funds to attend several local conventions of these industries. At the meetings, she entertained some key personnel of construction companies that had interests in her company's area. Eventually she concluded she had enough data to confirm her belief that, by inducing developers, architects, and contractors of large building projects to emphasize use of electric equipment and appliances, large increases in sales would result for her company. And the utility's profits would go up, even though some minor capital investments would be necessary.

Miss Wallace felt sure she would encounter inertia in her own department if she were to formally propose that the company undertake such a campaign. At the same time, she was convinced no serious harm would be done to the company if she moved cautiously on her own to interest several builders in her proposals. She had already consulted privately with acquaintances in her own company and was confident she knew how to proceed. Initially, she identified one large syndicate that was preparing to construct a complex of four high-rise apartment buildings. Through a friend, she made contact with a senior staff man in the syndicate and had several conversations with him. She became familiar with the builder's tentative plans concerning the size of the structures, the number of rental units involved, the types of units, the kinds of service that would be offered to tenants, and other pertinent information. She then made several trips to manufacturers of electrical equipment and appliances to determine their interest in the matter.

Miss Wallace now proceeded to develop a comprehensive presentation outlining the benefits that would result to the company from the kind of sales promotion program she had in mind. She was prepared to demonstrate how the company could provide inducements to the syndicate to seek bids from manufacturers of equipment and appliances for a completely electrified apartment complex. The incentives included favorable tariff and service proposals, and a plan to construct specific power supply units solely for the apartment buildings. Her plan also included methods the syndicate could use to stimulate interest on the part of manufacturers to bid on the job. Miss Wallace was in a position to reassure her superiors that all aspects of her plan were acceptable to the state utility commission, since she had gone to the capital herself to check that out.

Miss Wallace was now ready. She gave her immediate supervisor a general briefing on her proposal. She then requested, and received, permission to present her plan to the senior vice-president for marketing.

In examining the scope and nature of the authority acquired by Miss Wallace in this case, we find that she spent considerable time and used budgeted funds to evaluate a market (and develop a sales promotion approach) that the company had neither planned to exploit nor authorized anyone to explore. However, the area of authority into which she had moved was not too distant from the area of her formally delegated authority. Also, she had violated no explicit rules regarding the expenditure of funds, nor had she committed her company to any course of action. Yet it had required a significant degree of personal vision on Miss Wallace's part as to what was good for the company, a strong exercise of self-generated initiative, and the courage to propose breaking several company taboos. By her own efforts, she had now achieved a position from which she could point out to company management a direction in which to move in order to secure large increases in sales and profit.

Miss Wallace's plan was initially received by her principals—especially the vice-president—with a certain degree of shock. The president and chief executive officer heard about the plan almost immediately and, to almost everyone's surprise, he reacted very enthusiastically. He decided to involve himself personally in the first formal discussions with the syndicate. And he assigned to Miss Wallace the responsibility to coordinate the entire sales effort.

AUTHORITY ACQUIRED BY GIVING AWAY WORK

Joe Sidney was in charge of a special unit in the manufacturing department of a company that made construction and agricultural equipment. His shop produced small parts of unusual or special design, or parts with processing or treatment features that precluded their production in the department's regular manufacturing units. The parts he produced were seldom standard items of the type used in many different models of the company's products. Even so, they were not always produced in short runs. For some parts, the annual volume produced in the special shop was quite sizable.

Joe Sidney was held in high regard by the manufacturing superintendent, Brian Kent, who looked upon him as a very steady and dependable supervisor, capable of producing hard-to-make parts as economically as possible in this kind of job-shop operation. While Joe was aware of Brian's respect for him and his work, he had a quite different view of the economy and efficiency of his operation. As far as he was concerned, his shop was making many special items, in substantial quantities, which simply should not be manufactured at all by the company—or, at least, not in his shop. The reason he felt strongly about this was that his unit, because of its distinctive job-shop nature, tended to have considerably higher costs than the regular manufacturing units.

Joe had talked to Brian on several occasions about this uneconomical situation. He persisted in expressing the thought that the engineering people should be looking for ways to eliminate the special manufacturing requirements for many of the items produced in Joe's special shop. However, Brian was of the firm opinion that little could be done to improve and economize on the design and manufacture of those items.

Although Joe was a fairly slow mover, his convictions on this matter were so enduring that he eventually decided to look into the possibilities of applying value engineering to some of the items he produced. His purpose was to learn if value engineering techniques could be used to redesign parts so that they would fulfill their functions, but cost less to manufacture—the twin aims of value engineering. Joe was not an engineer, but he had acquired a certain amount of engineering knowledge by attending college courses at night. He had also taken a correspondence course in value analysis and was fairly well acquainted with the techniques, even though he had not yet put them into practice. He quietly arranged to attend a two-day seminar in value engineering in a nearby city to sharpen his practical understanding of the concepts and methods used.

Back in the shop, Joe then selected three different parts

from among his highest-volume items. They were also very expensive to manufacture in relation to the purposes they served in the equipments in which they were used. Joe went to a senior design engineer whom he knew, someone he considered to be open-minded and imaginative. They discussed the parts, examined the drawings and specifications, and looked at the actual physical assemblies in which the parts were used. Joe then went into the assembly shop and spoke to several supervisors who were well acquainted with the equipment in which these parts were used and with the assembly processes involved. He also spoke to a maintenance expert in the service planning department regarding maintenance and replacement problems associated with the parts and assemblies. By then, he was convinced that two of the three items could be redesigned in such a way that they would be simpler and much less costly to produce. Not only would they be highly satisfactory in operation, but they would simplify the maintenance problem. (While all this activity required a considerable effort on Joe's part, he was, of course, still devoting enough time to his own shop to keep it operating properly.)

He then took the initiative to prepare a request for an engineering design project covering the two items he thought could be improved. He convinced the design unit supervisor to initiate the project and assign it to Joe's senior engineering friend. Joe and the engineer worked together and came up with what Joe considered to be highly economical and efficient design specifications and production orders. He personally approved a shop order, in his own unit, to run off a small lot of each of the two items. He took the finished parts to the assembly shop and talked the superintendent there into putting them into several of the assemblies in which they were used. These equipments were then run up on the testing facilities. Both revised items exceeded all design and maintenance specifications.

Joe then went to the purchasing department. With the help of a senior buyer, he checked through the department's reference files to find some parts suppliers who were likely sources for these items since, in their redesigned form, they were not radically different from common, standard parts available from regular supply companies. After much telephone research, Joe and the buyer found a supplier for one of the parts and spoke to him about an order for the item. Joe estimated that his company would save about $35,000 a year by buying this redesigned part instead of specially manufacturing it in house.

Regarding the second item that was redesigned through the use of value engineering, Joe was not satisfied with the prices offered by suppliers. He checked back with the regular parts manufacturing units in his company. He was told that the department could make the redesigned part at a favorable cost, compared to outside suppliers, and at a savings of about $20,000 a year when measured against the complicated part previously produced in Joe's shop. With the concurrence of the assembly department, Joe arranged for the in-house manufacture of a three months' supply of the part.

At this point, he thought he had better talk to his boss, Bill Petrie, the assistant superintendent of the manufacturing department. He wanted to tell him about what he had done and urge him to continue this type of value engineering review on a number of other parts designated for manufacture by Joe's unit. When Joe and his boss met, the essence of the conversation went something like this:

Boss: I heard you were visiting around the department, asking questions, and running some tests over in assembly. I didn't bother to ask you about it, but somebody said it looked like you were trying to unload some of your work.

Joe: Well, I guess I am in a way, Bill. You know as well as I do that my shop is about the most expensive place you can go to get parts. All I'm trying to do is use value engineering to save some money for the company.

Boss: I know a little about value engineering. You mean you've really hit on something?

Joe: That's right. We've looked at these three parts that we make—high-volume items. Bill, on two of them we can save over $50,000 a year! I already have a supplier lined up for one part. On the other item, the regular parts production shop has already started work on a small order. Now, I admit we can't expect to save that much on every part we look at, but I say that there's an awful lot of money to be made on this idea.

Boss: I'll have to look at it, Joe. It sounds really good. But, listen, you know that engineering could raise hell about us getting into their area, if we keep doing this value engineering business over in your shop.

Joe: But I'm not looking for that kind of work as a steady diet, Bill. I'm just trying to sell this idea—looking at the parts I'm producing to see if we can redesign them. Make it simpler, less expensive—and get it from somewhere outside my shop. *I'll* still have plenty of work to do. Anyway, I've been coordinating this with engineering and we worked on it together.

Boss: O.K., Joe, I'll tell you what. I'm going to ask the super if it's all right to set up a working arrangement with engineering. If Brian Kent approves it, I'll see to it that you have the responsibility to head up the program—for a while, anyway, until it really gets going.

So, we see how Joe Sidney had an idea that he was convinced would make money for the company. The idea involved a new approach that touched his area of authority, but was perhaps more outside the area than in it. Yet he had the initiative to carry it through. He took the responsibility for the effort, and showed considerable success with it. Finally, he actually was delegated the authority to run the program, at least through its formative stages. This is a good example of going through the classic sequence of getting an idea, using personal initiative forcefully, acquiring responsibility and authority, achieving success, then, at last, receiving a formal delegation of the previously acquired authority.

A CRITICAL BOSS SEES THE LIGHT

Authority is not always acquired without some degree of adversity. The cynics often stand in the way, ready to question the motives of those who seek to use initiative to do something worthwhile for the company. Reactionaries are encountered—those who oppose change that does not occur at a measured pace by way of the "right" channels. And there are other types of people with a variety of reasons for being critical when they discover that someone has used initiative to assume administrative power. Thus the man who seeks to acquire authority without encountering any criticism whatsoever may never reach that goal.

In this instance, Stanley Lewis found that he had to overcome criticism, just short of ridicule, in order to achieve success in expanding his authority. Furthermore, his experience demonstrates that sheer opportunism is not always enough in seeking undelegated authority. As is the case in many other aspects of achievement in business, Lewis, in this case, had to be prepared ahead of time for the chance to acquire authority. In fact, as we shall see, he had a great deal to do with shaping the circumstances under which he was able to reach for, and grasp, the power he sought to use for the company's benefit.

Lewis was a senior engineer and team leader in a consulting firm. He was usually assigned as the head of a team involved in the company's most complex projects. A very active and alert leader, he was very much interested in his work. He liked the company, even though he was occasionally frustrated by its rather conservative approach to management.

Having reached his senior position several years earlier, Lewis frequently made suggestions and attempted to carry out tasks beyond the scope of his assignments. To his way of thinking, a readiness to reach out and do more than the minimum seemed to be a rational mode of action for a man in his position. He considered this approach to an assignment as a way that would provide a better result for the customers and would certainly be of benefit to his company. He found, however, that under the company's very tight control system, there was so much observation and monitoring of project status that his efforts to use his initiative were always detected early in the game. The result was frequent criticism from his boss about the effort Lewis was expending on tasks outside the specifications of the project.

On one occasion, after Lewis had spent the morning helping the engineering department of a client company to solve a scheduling problem, his boss needled him at lunch. Several other senior engineers of the consulting firm were also at the table. The boss pointed out that the scheduling problem had nothing to do with their project of setting up a processing line for the client, which was what they were being paid to do. He asked jokingly if Lewis were thinking of going into business for himself.

Lewis was convinced that his boss was being shortsighted. Although he liked him well enough, he felt that his boss somehow had to be made to realize that Lewis was not going to limit himself to a narrow definition of his duties. He was willing to risk the boss's needling and criticism again. However, to get maximum protection against the risks involved, he decided that next time he would select a situation in his own favor to demonstrate his initiative in acquiring responsibility and authority beyond the specific scope of his job.

Lewis's next chance came soon enough. He became aware that his boss had just been assigned a new, unwanted, and troublesome function. He heard, through the grapevine, that his boss would temporarily carry out the new duties until he had time to decide which of his team leaders should be assigned the task.

Lewis's boss was concerned about his sudden dilemma: the nature of the new function was such that he was sure all his supervisors would object to the assignment. He was reluctant to allocate the job against the wishes of the supervisor he might select. The job involved carrying out a followup, with clients, on the projects the consulting firm had completed for them. The object was to determine what problems they were running into in implementing the firm's recommendations. The task involved a lot of work, as well as the probability that the assigned supervisor would be the immediate target for criticism whenever the customer indicated anything less than a high level of acceptance of the company's recommendations in action. In any case, this new service for customers promised to be a profitable source of additional business for the firm.

Lewis recognized that the assignment had a low potential for bringing credit to the man doing the job. However, after

studying the situation, he quickly set out to contact personally a number of clients for whom his firm had completed
consulting projects in recent months. He did not mention his
activity in this area to his boss, but made sure *not* to get in
touch with any clients his boss was contacting. After checking with five customers and discussing with them the service offered and the fee schedule, he initiated various actions that were helpful to each of them.

Upon completing these self-appointed tasks, Lewis wrote
a report to his boss concerning the progress he had made.
The boss was somewhat taken aback that Lewis had assumed this responsibility on his own. However, he quickly
recognized that this solved the dilemma as to whom he
should assign the function. He therefore gracefully made it
official that Lewis had the function, and gave him the authority to carry on with it. Thus while the actual performance of the task itself might not bring much credit to
Lewis, the initiative he showed in seizing the responsibility
to do it marked him as a man willing to go out of his way to
benefit the company under difficult circumstances. He also
felt that, by not limiting himself to a narrow definition of his
duties, he had made his point regarding the company benefits to be accrued by such action.

NO BUSINESS LIKE NEW BUSINESS

Jim Schwartz did not believe that his boss expected him to
operate within sharply defined limits. As a salesman, his
creed was that if you don't move forward, you will surely fall
back. Jim was a supervisor in the sales department of a
well-established company that manufactured a wide variety
of industrial motors, pumps, and allied products. His section
of salesmen usually exceeded their sales quotas by a
higher percentage than any other section in the department.

Jim not only was very demanding of his men, but he also
exerted a great deal of personal effort to make it possible
for them to achieve high sales volume. One effort, in particular, was the building up of close personal relationships
with supervisors and officials in other departments of the
company, such as manufacturing, purchasing, and account-

ing. He was well known for his tactics of persuading and needling his acquaintances in such a way as to convince them to take action that would help his salesmen to get orders, to promise deliveries on short schedules, and to offer other favorable features to customers.

His immediate boss, George Luce, vice-president for marketing, was aware of Jim's very active initiative, but he had mixed feelings about his somewhat aggressive leadership style. He was always very pleased with Jim's results; but he was also somewhat fearful that, because Jim sometimes took liberties in the process of using his initiative, he might bring down on the head of the sales department the wrath of other members of top management. However, he was also aware that Jim was an accomplished diplomat and, so far, had always managed to muffle the potential complaints of those who might object to his mode of operation.

As an example of Jim's kind of initiative, in one week he handled two different orders in ways that caused his boss some consternation when he heard about them. In one case, to insure that one of his salesmen would get a very large and profitable order, Jim personally approved the quoting of a unit price that was 5 percent below the lowest price he was currently allowed to offer. Before making the low offer, he checked with a friend in the accounting department. He found that this would be the largest order for this item in two years, and that the cost pattern on the item was such that, even at the very low price, a higher profit per unit than normal would result from the volume.

In the second case, Jim was concerned that the manufacturing department would not be able to meet a promised delivery date for an emergency shipment to an excellent customer. The delay factor was slippage in the receipt of needed parts from one of the company's suppliers. Jim checked with the purchase department and was told that their best efforts to expedite delivery of the parts by the supplier were to no avail. Jim then called a friend in a local bank and had him make a few telephone calls to determine the principal banking connection of the supplier. Through a contact in the supplier's bank, it was learned that the supplier was in a firm financial position, but, because of current limitations on his cash position, had sharply reduced over-time operations for the current period. Jim then called the assistant head of his own company's accounting depart-ment, who gave his grudging approval of an advance pay-ment to the supplier. Jim contacted the appropriate official in the supplier's company and advised him that an advance payment would be forthcoming if the supplier went on over-time to produce the needed parts quickly. The supplier agreed.

Jim's performance in these two cases represented the high-water mark (up to this point) of his activity in assuming authority in cases where he felt it would be beneficial to the company. He actually went considerably beyond his as-signed functional responsibilities in both instances. To a no-ticeable extent, he invaded functional areas assigned to other departments. He got away with it, probably because he checked beforehand with the responsible department in each case. In offering a unit price reduction, Jim made sure that there were grounds for a lower price—that is, the order was larger than any other ever experienced for this item, and the profit situation justified the lower cost. In the case of expediting parts to insure that a promised delivery schedule would be met, Jim made certain that the purchase department had exhausted all possible solutions that it was aware of. Furthermore, he secured the accounting depart-ment's approval for the advance payment that induced the supplier to go on an overtime basis. By taking positive steps to clear his proposed actions beforehand with all depart-ments involved, the result was that Jim used his acquired authority in a manner that did not confuse the structure of delegated authority, but that did result in substantial benefit to the company.

Although he gained some hesitant praise for his initiative in those two cases, Jim was well aware that his wheeling-and-dealing tactics were causing some discomfiture to his boss and to some managers in other departments. He de-cided that if he went much further in the direction of assum-ing the authority of other departments, the reaction could be painful to him and traumatic to his boss. Nevertheless, Jim felt certain that it would be wasteful to the company if he did not assume power where it was available and useful, and, hopefully, without infringing very much on the authority of others in the company.

In recent months, Jim had become somewhat concerned about the possibility that sales potential for the company was gradually softening. While overall sales volume was increasing, it was increasing at a diminishing rate. Also, the difference between actual sales volume and projected sales potential was decreasing. Jim was convinced that the company's efforts to increase the size and depth of the market were inadequate. He felt this was the primary reason for the danger signals he detected. The means for turning this situation around, he was certain, was a vigorous program for attracting new business.

No one in the company was really responsible for a new business program, as such. The advertising department carried out various promotion programs, but the new business efforts were diffused. The company relied on various uncoordinated campaigns for attracting customers—such as ads in trade publications, shared-cost local advertising with dealers, exhibits at industrial conventions, and the offering of special inducements to dealers to increase their local sales effort. The company sold its products directly to customers who used them and to retail distributors. There were two important types of direct customers: the manufacturers of heavy equipment in which the products of the company were incorporated as part of the finished equipment, and the large industrial users of the motors, pumps, and other items produced by the company.

Jim was satisfied that there would be a low risk of damage if he experimented with a small pilot operation in seeking new business. He assured himself that his plan did not include any features that could be interpreted as trespassing into the advertising department's territory, or anyone else's, for that matter. He knew of no specific company policies that he would contravene with his test operation. Finally, he decided that under the circumstances, he didn't really have to notify his boss of what he was doing until he had some results to show him.

Jim assigned his two best salesmen to the test program

for increasing new business. They would operate the program in their own sales territories on a part-time basis. The major elements of the program are described below.

Direct soliciting of potential customers who had never used the company's products. Jim spent several hundred dollars to buy (from a market research agency) a special listing of manufacturing companies and other firms in the test areas that could be classified as potential customers.

Offering engineering know-how to interested customers, old and new, to solve design problems, product applications, and so on. The aim of this effort was to demonstrate that the company's line would prove to be useful and profitable in the customer's situation. Also, the salesmen offered to arrange for the company's products to be tailored to fit the customer's needs.

Making offers to all companies contacted to arrange for expedited delivery and other special services, based on order size and other favorable considerations.

Contacting by salesmen those people and firms who were not potential customers themselves, but who might influence current and potential customers. In this element of the program, contact was made with banks, industrial maintenance companies, engineering consultant firms, plant architects and builders, industrial designers, and the like.

Jim had many other ideas for the new business campaign, which he refrained from using. The reason was that implementation of the ideas would go beyond the bounds of the two salesmen's territories and would be profitable only if applied on a wider regional base.

After a six months' operation of the pilot program for new business, dollar sales in the two test sales territories increased by 30 percent and 40 percent, respectively. Of course, the two salesmen involved were Jim's best. However, he calculated that with an even broader and more professional full-time new business program, an average annual increase in sales of 25 percent across-the-board could easily be sustained for a number of years in an ever increasing market. This would entail a moderate and quite acceptable increase in sales expense.

It was now time for Jim to break the good news to his

boss (George Luce, the vice-president for marketing), who was only minimally aware of certain aspects of the test program. Jim arranged (through the boss's administrative assistant) for a meeting with Mr. Luce and his top staff people, at which Jim planned to make a presentation on the program. He reasoned that the best tactics to adopt for his pitch were: to concentrate on the statistical information that described the pilot program; to emphasize that he had carried out a test only; to highlight the successful results and the projected results from a full-time program; and to avoid even the slightest mention of authority, either acquired or delegated. At the end of the presentation, he would propose an immediate moderate expansion of the pilot, with no recommendation as to who would be responsible for the program in the future.

Jim polished his material and, one pleasant morning—taking along the two salesmen who had carried out the trial program—he made his presentation in Mr. Luce's conference room. Here is an excerpt from the initial portion of the meeting.

Mr. Luce: Jim, what you told my assistant about the subject of this get-together doesn't give me much of a clue . . . something about new business. We've been wondering what it's all about. Good news, I hope!

Jim: Well, George, it's just an idea we had in my shop, an approach to increasing sales that we'd like to get your reaction on. We did a small test of the concept, on a pilot basis, just to check out the possibilities before we bothered you with it. I have some slides with me. I'd appreciate the opportunity to summarize the program and see what you gentlemen think of it.

Mr. Luce: Sure, let's have it, Jim. It sounds interesting. I'm putting two and two together here. If I know you, I'm prepared to bet that this project isn't as small as you're trying to make it out. Not only that, but this has got to be the explanation of why you've been too busy to put your well-known heat on some of the other departments. I haven't received any complaints about that lately. All right, Jim, fine. Go ahead.

(We break away from the excerpt at this point, as Jim

starts his prepared presentation. After twenty minutes, he concludes his pitch. There were practically no questions during the presentation itself. We return to the excerpt, as Jim prepares to field his boss's comments.)

Mr. Luce: Well, Jim, give me just a minute to absorb this. I guess you noticed how quiet I was during your presentation. I'm not sure whether that's because it was so interesting or because I was stunned by what you've done! It seems to me you came pretty close to overcommitting me in this operation without even mentioning it. But I'll let that pass for the time being. At least, it doesn't seem that you got me and the marketing group into any serious trouble—so far, anyway! Now what convinced you that this is anything more than a one-shot spectacular? Why should the company spend a lot more money on this kind of a marginal promotion approach?

Jim: George, in our planning and execution of this concept, we never for a minute regarded it as anything but a test of a full-scale program for increasing our market on a permanent basis! There's no one-time aspect to it at all. The entire orientation of the pilot was to step up to a new level of marketing our products. Remember, we pushed this program in the field for six months before we came to see you about it. I can tell you that we've been back to some of our contacts on three separate occasions. And each time we had a wider impact, in terms of exposing new customers to our line. And notice this, George—in the sales territories involved, you can't even notice the increase in sales cost. It's minimal! It's not a question of spending a lot of money. It's not a matter of a marginal program. We demonstrated what kind of results you can expect if we change our vision of what our market is.

Mr. Luce: Jim, you're telling me we've been wrong all these years, all this time that we have had a sound, profitable position in the industry. Are you seriously questioning our past history of performance?

Jim: Not a bit, sir. We got where we are by hard work and high quality. That's the hallmark of our products. So what do we do—coast along with our old customers? I say we've got to broadcast our products and services to other people who don't already know what we have to offer. That's all we tried to do in our pilot—reach more firms who aren't familiar with our products. That's the basic idea. Could anyone possibly quarrel with that proposition?

Mr. Luce: Jim, none of us here questions your motives. What you've done is valuable to the company. It's a different look at how we approach the customer. But you know that management here takes a conservative view on expansion. If I give you all-out support on this, it's going to look like a whole new ball game to the president—and the board, too. *We* like it. It looks wholesome to us. But it will look revolutionary to *them,* especially since they don't know anything about it. If we go in with a full-blown proposition to expand in this direction, the boss will want to give it a lot of consideration. I'm sure he'll decide he has to get a reaction from the directors. I'm afraid it will stall out. It could lose its momentum.

Jim: Sir, we've taken a little step, so far. All we need at this time is a few more short steps. Let's not ask the president to approve the whole program at this time. You'll remember that in my presentation, I proposed we go ahead with a moderate expansion of the pilot. That's all you ought to seek approval on at this time, I think. Just a full pilot program, to test the concept. Don't you think the boss could be approached on that basis—with the suggestion that he could approve that without involving the board? It would still be just a test.

Mr. Luce: Well, yes, I see your point, Jim. I think so. I think you have the right approach there. I could do that. Listen, Jim, what we need is a proposal that puts it right in the president's bailiwick—a pitch like you gave us today, with a proposal to conduct a wider test that won't involve any substantial increase in cost. If we talk about another $20,000 or $30,000, he won't visualize it as any major commitment. You can do it, can't you? I'll make the pitch to him and you be there to back me up. I'll tell him that you're just the man to run this full-scale test. Do you think you could oversee the test without bringing somebody else in to supervise your section?

Jim: Of course I can, George. That sounds excellent! If

you want me to run the test, I'll be glad to help out. It's no problem. Most of the other sales managers already know something about the program. They like it. I'll put together a proposed pitch for you to give the president. And I'll draft a letter to sales supervisors, which you can sign if he approves the expanded test. It will outline the program and ask them for their continued cooperation, with me as temporary program director. Is that what you had in mind?

Mr. Luce: That sounds good, Jim. Let's go ahead along those lines.

This case, and the others in this chapter, demonstrate a few of the varied approaches to acquiring authority. There are many avenues and many techniques for assuming and using administrative power in a manner that will favorably affect operations. They all have this in common: With the right motives, it is usually possible for the individual manager to acquire authority on his own initiative and to use it in a way that ultimately benefits the company and himself.

7 * MANAGEMENT'S ROLE IN THE ACQUISITION OF AUTHORITY

A company that wishes to profit from the acquisition of authority by its managers must have a policy of deliberate and overt encouragement of such activity. Those who seek to acquire power in a company whose management displays a neutral or even a negative attitude are made to feel like administrative guerillas. Their initiative is diluted in a running battle with management. If a company is not going to participate actively by urging its members to acquire authority, the best course of action may be to advertise the fact that only the authority that is delegated will be exercised.

For the company that is convinced it will benefit from the use of acquired authority by its managers, there are many means by which top management and the upper echelon of supervision can actively spread the gospel of initiative in action. These means should all be characterized by their practicality and obvious connection with company progress. The overall objective of top management effort in this direction should be to foster a definite climate of acceptance of this fundamental idea: The company anticipates that managers will seek to broaden their individual administrative power, in an acceptable way, for the company's benefit as well as their own. This chapter discusses how to achieve such a climate in a practical way.

THE FORMAL ORGANIZATION IS
NOT SACRED

Insistence on strict adherence to the formal organization structure can have a deadly effect on stifling a manager's enterprise. The natural growth pattern of managers and the vitality of the company itself usually engender a strong pressure for change and expansion. To accommodate this phenomenon, management should be alert to the need to alter its structure. Furthermore, it is often desirable to change the formal organization structure so that it conforms with the actual distribution of functional power (which may have changed considerably) rather than vice versa.

Management that chooses to reject this enlightened approach, and refuses to tolerate any activity that does not appear in approved organizational or functional statements, had better be prepared to exercise eternal vigilance in stamping out deviations, or to quickly make them legal by issuing formal approval. Even where the climate for growth is negative, it is virtually impossible to entirely eliminate the inner drive toward expansion of power.

The first commandment, then, in a program of encouraging the acquisition of authority by managers is: *Don't preach or practice rigid adherence to the formal organization structure of the company.* Top management not only must profess belief in the flexibility of the organization, but must also provide positive evidence of this belief through its actions. Obviously, this does not mean that organizational anarchy should be preached. It does mean, however, that care must be exercised not to give even the appearance of dominance by the organizational structure. An executive who justifies a negative decision regarding a proposal for action on the basis that it is not in keeping with the official organization chart is certainly not promoting a climate of acceptance.

A logical expansion of this thought leads to a second commandment for encouraging the acquisition of authority: *To the greatest extent possible, don't restrict the actions of supervisors on the grounds that such limitations are dictated by the company's official organization structure or distribution of functions.*

Beyond these general principles that management should apply to encourage acquisition of authority, there are specific and concrete measures that can be practiced. A variety of everyday actions, all quite feasible and effective, can be programmed and scheduled for routine execution. For example, the training or indoctrination courses sponsored by the company should stress that formal organization and functional assignments represent mainly the basic guidelines for the distribution of authority. It should be emphasized that they do not represent absolute limits or exclusive territorial franchises. Courses, seminars, or meetings conducted under company auspices are normally presumed by managers to have official sanction. Therefore, any statement made through such media is usually interpreted as a statement of company policy. Hence, these gatherings offer an excellent opportunity to present the company's views on the use of initiative to take action in areas not specifically delegated to someone.

An allied technique for encouraging managers to abandon provincial tendencies is to take advantage of programs for cross-assigning promising executives to departments outside their original areas of specialization. Such programs are carried out by many companies as a way of indoctrinating managers in company operations. As part of such a program, a deliberate effort can be undertaken to urge participants to exercise the authority inherent in the departments to which they are temporarily assigned. This presents an opportunity to make the point that the manager is capable of using authority with sufficient facility to achieve improvements, even outside his own area of specialization.

The most positive and aggressive method for a company to use in demonstrating its belief that the formal organization is not sacred is to make specific assignments to managers that will forcefully take them somewhat outside their areas of delegated authority. By this technique, management does more than merely place a mantle of respectability over a manager's inherent drive to move outside his personal bailiwick. In effect, it is pushing him, or demanding him, to cross the line. There are many readily available devices for doing this, such as special assignments, designation to a task group or committee, or a project assignment ostensibly within the manager's area of functional responsibility but with objectives that require him to go afield from his own component. Management is almost always in a position to use these outgoing techniques with little danger of fouling the lines of authority, because it is relatively easy to plan the scope of assignments in a way that will prevent serious intrusion on established areas of authority.

DON'T STIFLE THE EXERCISE
OF INITIATIVE

There is a direct correlation between the number of significant actions taken by managers (such as making decisions, guiding subordinates, taking action to improve some aspect of productivity) and the level of company performance. With a given group of competent managers, an increase in the number of such management actions generally produces more benefits for the company. As a second link in this chain of reasoning, it can be said that the volume of significant action taken by managers depends on the amount of actual authority they put to use. In summary, then, authority makes the manager, and the manager makes the difference in company success.

On the basis of such logic, the third commandment in encouraging acquisition of authority can be stated as follows: *Do not unnecessarily impede a manager from exercising his initiative to carry out worthwhile activities, even though they may extend beyond the normal limits of his delegated authority.*

One way of measuring a company's success in encouraging initiative—and making more effective use of authority —is to evaluate the status of four key indicators regarding decision making. In general, effective use of authority in a company is more pronounced:

□ The greater the number of decisions made lower down in the organization structure.

□ The more important the decisions made lower down in the organization structure.

□ The greater the number of functions or systems affected by decisions made low in the organization structure.

□ The less checking required on these decisions by higher authority.

These four criteria are indicative of what to expect when authority is applied in a climate of vigorous initiative. When the use of acquired authority is encouraged, a company can expect to earn very high marks in an examination of its decision-making process.

Those who are no longer novices in the field of management have perhaps forgotten what it is like to be a new manager. What factors, good or bad, are faced by younger members of management in their adventuresome efforts to seek administrative power, especially when they use initiative to acquire authority? For one thing, men learn to manage by *being* managers. The typical good manager gains skill in applying the authority delegated to him in a relatively short period of time, when the period is measured against the total number of years of his entire career as manager. Each time he moves to a higher level of authority, the learning curve for gaining proficiency in the use of his new power is flatter, and he climbs it quicker. At each new level, he soon becomes restive if confined within the area of his delegated authority. If he is made to stay within those limits, he tends to overmanage his functions and his people just to keep busy. But if the acquisition of authority is encouraged, the manager finds early in his career that his initiative can provide new worlds to conquer soon after he has his delegated authority well in control. In a liberal atmosphere, he learns that authority gives him many opportunities:

□ To make decisions about matters that have not been dictated by others.

□ To interpret the meaning of policies or procedures that *have* been laid down by those higher in the organization.

▫ To determine the kinds of action to be taken by himself and by others. And, finally,

▫ To stretch his initiative. The manager can frequently go beyond the limits of what he has been told he must do, and move into zones he has not been forbidden to enter— especially into areas where his efforts are most likely to produce benefits for the company.

An excellent move for the enterprise seeking to take a positive course for insuring that the managers' initiative is not stifled is to express its attitude to all executives and supervisors. For example, it should be made clear that officials are to avoid acting in an automatic, negative way whenever they discover a subordinate in the process of acquiring or exercising authority not specifically delegated to him. Rather, each instance is to be evaluated on its own merits, and the official is to be guided by his findings.

ACCEPT MISTAKES WITH PERSPECTIVE

One way of looking at errors committed in a company is to regard them as a normal and acceptable cost of doing business—up to a point, of course. From another standpoint, it is sometimes more profitable to accept a certain percentage of error than to strive for perfection. (The elimination of those last few percentage points of error may bankrupt the company.)

These two views, which offer practical and demonstrable advantages as viable attitudes toward the cost of doing business, are acceptable to most executives. Often, unfortunately, this same kind of understanding and acceptance are not exhibited in the case of errors committed when managers do something that has not received prior management approval. This raises a pertinent question: Why should there be harsh penalties against incorrect actions resulting from the exercise of someone's initiative?

The question leads to the fourth commandment in encouraging acquisition of authority: *Don't chastise a manager simply on the basis that he committed an error while ex-*

ceeding his authority. If a supervisor makes a mistake while somewhat afield of his area of delegated authority and he gets into trouble as a result, he should be informed that acquisition of authority in the company's cause is not wrong in itself, as long as it is kept within certain acceptable bounds. These limits should be explained to him and an effort made to describe to him, as explicitly as possible, the correct action that should have been taken in those particular circumstances.

The occurrence of errors does not alter the fact that different kinds and degrees of acquisition of authority can exist, some of which are acceptable, and some not. In any case, the question of acceptability of a manager's acquisition of power should never be judged on the basis of whether or not he committed an error while exercising his initiative. Naturally, if a manager feels compelled to stay in line, follow directions, and not venture into new territory, there is little likelihood of major mistakes. Unfortunately, this also decreases the chances that the company will benefit from major advances through creative management. Errors of action, in themselves, should not damn the manager. He should be held strictly accountable, however, for errors of judgment that take him into territory where the odds for success are obviously against him.

PUBLICIZE THE COMPANY'S INITIATIVE

The kind of encouragement most impressive to a manager seeking to be aggressive in a constructive way is the example set by the company. The enthusiastic manager is reinforced in his motivation to gain and use power advantageously by any aggressive action the company takes as an entity—to seek new markets and new product lines, to move into a better competitive position, to undertake new endeavors, and so on. The point is, if it makes sense for the company to "move out," then it makes sense for the manager to do so, too. Enterprise and innovation are laudable activities for the company to undertake, and they are also beneficial for the company when carried out by individual supervisors or executives.

Top management is almost always in a position to have some control over exactly how and when employees are to be informed of company success. Such an event is an important one, and should not be treated simply as an occasion for the straightforward dissemination of news. It is an opportunity for demonstrating company intent and objectives, and for explaining just what the company seeks and sanctions in the way of progress. In spreading the news, management should have as a principal goal the proper guidance and motivation of its employees. As far as media are concerned, all accepted means of informing employees are useful—for instance, house organs, flash newsletters, letters to managers and/or other company personnel, and meetings. Again, the point is to get the message to managers in such a way that it is not only news, but a reaffirmation of the company's belief that its members should extend themselves to make progress. Thus the fifth commandment in encouraging acquisition of authority is: *Don't neglect to advertise those situations in which the company has acted aggressively to move beyond previously defined areas of interest.*

GIVE RESPONSIBILITY TO
THE HIGHEST BIDDER

Management action in encouraging manager acquisition of authority obviously requires the exercise of discretion. Everything the company believes and practices in the area of authority does not necessarily have to be stated in an outspoken way; it is possible to get the word out in an indirect fashion. For example, the company may wish to spread the message that in certain areas where it is not feasible to assign responsibility specifically to an individual, the authority associated with that responsibility is open for acquisition. Management's objective here is to make it known that whoever wants the responsibility can pick it up and run with it—or—whoever is eager for power can attempt to acquire it. Of course, there should always be an explicit and firm requirement accompanying this sort of underground message that such acquisition, first, must be to the company's benefit; second, must be legal; third, must not infringe on the rights and responsibilities of others to their detriment.

In the above description of management action, note that emphasis is placed on responsibility first, and authority second. A sound principle to follow, when a discreet stance by the company is desirable, is to stress acquired responsibility. This mode of action provides a natural brake on the potential empire-builder and the self-seeking adventurer.

A manager who is forced to face up initially to a sense of responsibility for what he does feels the weight of that burden, which acts as a counterbalance for the exhilaration of newly gained authority. It should certainly be made clear, by example and precept, that management looks unfavorably upon the irresponsible acquisition of authority. From management's standpoint, it is an important measure of the manager (especially in sensitive areas of authority, where poor judgment can be substantially harmful to the company) when he takes a conscientious view of his responsibility.

On this basis, the sixth commandment that management should follow in advocating the assumption of administrative power is: *Where authority is available for acquisition, don't fail to emphasize that, all other things being equal, management favors the man who shows the greatest inclination toward fully shouldering the responsibility involved.* This sort of standard is an acid test—a test of the man's sincerity, indicating that he is not frivolous or self-seeking in terms of wanting authority for its own sake.

REWARD THE ACQUIRER OF AUTHORITY

A policy that encourages the acquisition of authority by qualified persons, and under the right conditions, is advocated for virtually every company. However, it must be recognized that the acquisition of authority is not totally its own reward. Moreover, once authority is firmly acquired by a manager, it can become dangerous if allowed to go on unrecognized by management. Hence, the seventh and last commandment for encouraging the assumption of authority is: *Don't let the beneficial acquisition of authority go unrewarded and unprotected.*

When acquired authority has proved to be beneficial to the enterprise, the company can provide a basic contribution by making that authority legitimate. If someone has acquired authority that was not delegated, and has proven in practice that this is a good and useful circumstance for the company, then such authority should be recognized. In addition (though not necessarily always), the authority should be protected and made permanent under the mantle of official and formal delegation. This process has many purposes:

◻ It removes that particular authority from the arena of possible dissension and argument as to who should have rightful possession of it.

◻ It gives recognition to the man with the initiative to have acquired it, plus the sense of responsibility to use it to the benefit of the company.

◻ It firmly fixes the fact that this is a regularized function of the company, thus permitting the official acknowledgment, funding, and support of the authority (which now has official status).

◻ It informs those above the acquiring manager in the vertical line of organization that this power is now within their range of authority, if they did not already know this.

◻ It maintains this authority in its rightful place in the organization, in the event that the man who created the authority unofficially should move on to another position or company.

◻ It gives status and encouragement to those who are inclined toward acquiring authority on their own.

As we shall see later, there are many means by which management can maintain watchfulness over the acquisition of authority and be aware as to when, where, and how it was acquired. The point here is that management can and should take action to incorporate acquired authority into the formal power structure. Once the acquired authority has been identified and shown to be useful, it should be capitalized upon to insure that continuing advantage is taken of it. It can simply be moved into the regular authority structure by using the same methods employed in the normal, ordinary course of formally delegating authority.

Unless there are very special reasons for doing otherwise, the official delegation of authority should be made to the man who acquired it initially. By this means, he is not penalized or discouraged as a result of his action. If, for some reason, it is not possible to officially delegate the authority to its initial acquirer, it may be better to simply dissolve it rather than delegate it to someone else. After a decent interval, it may be possible to resurrect and reassign the acquired authority, in the guise of formally delegated authority, to someone else. An effort should be made to prevent this from being painfully evident to the man who struggled to acquire it in the first instance.

What should management do, in terms of recognizing effort and initiative in acquiring authority, beyond formalizing the acquirer's grip on that power? A significant answer is that it would certainly be wasteful to ignore such favorable activity in evaluating a man's performance and promotability. (More is said about this factor in Chapter 9.) A triumph in the exercise of initiative can be indicative of a manager's potential for playing a more important role in company management.

How can we really judge a man's performance in regard to acquired authority? It should be judged in the same way that the exercise of *delegated* authority is measured (recognizing, of course, that extra credit for initiative may be warranted). The parallel exists with regard to *control* of acquired authority, as well. (Again, we shall see later on how the controls available for delegated authority can be used effectively for acquired authority.)

CREATE A FAVORABLE CLIMATE

To crystallize top management's function in the acquisition of authority by its managers, it can be said that it is a matter of creating an attitude and a willingness to loosen the grip over authority that normally prevails in the process of strict delegation. For most managers, the tendency toward or away from the exercise of initiative in acquiring power is strongly influenced by management's evident attitude. Where a strong authoritarian climate exists in the company, most men (including managers) prefer to be directed, and their ambitions become limited. However, in a situation where centralized control and direction are not exercised with a heavy hand (for either positive or negative reasons), the average manager tends to exercise his imagination, ingenuity, and drive for authority through self-direction and self-control. Thus the climate of the company (perhaps even more than the personality of the manager) is very influential in dictating the degree of activity to be found in the area of acquired authority.

In general, where the climate is right, managers seek to become responsible and to exercise authority. Top management, therefore, has a clear-cut choice, and an evident course of action to follow, in pursuing its vision of what can be accomplished by encouraging the acquisition of authority.

8 * IMPROVING THE PATTERN OF AUTHORITY

When top executives come to recognize authority as an important factor in company success they find themselves faced with the significant question of how to achieve and maintain an effective *pattern* of authority. In the many possible answers to this question (some of which are discussed here), several fundamental themes are predominant: The distribution of authority should be a flexible process; it should involve substantial, rather than nominal, power; it should be related to, and result in, high performance.

In every company, many factors are at play to influence the exact configuration of the power pattern at any given time. This phenomenon of an animated authority structure should be accepted as a dynamic fact of life in an organization. The pattern, however, should not be allowed to grow and change without some degree of observation. A continuing and familiar knowledge of the actual pattern of authority serves as the basis for constructive effort to improve it, and makes it possible to control undesirable trends and movements. Even more important, it expands the opportunity to support—or, at least, demonstrate permissive acceptance of—favorable modifications in the authority structure.

The preceding chapters dealt with the roles of the manager and the company in increasing the volume and quantity of applied power through the use of acquired authority. The discussion here covers both delegated and acquired authority—the entire range of the company's administrative power—and how the company can improve the overall pattern of distribution of authority. This type of improvement is of great practical significance. It can lead directly to an increase in dollar payoff, in terms of accelerated development of managers and positive contribution to company advancement.

GUIDELINES FOR EFFECTIVE DISTRIBUTION OF AUTHORITY

Some of the basic precepts and techniques for effective distribution of authority are now stated, with a brief discussion of each. (It should be noted that several of these guidelines are examined elsewhere in the book in greater detail and in a somewhat different context.) This extensive listing should serve to emphasize the wide range of tools available for shaping administrative power into an effective force for company progress.

Delegated and acquired authority should be meaningful in terms of the power it generates. The possession of authority means little, unless real power and substance are attached to it. Meaningful authority is that which enables a manager to cause significant things to happen. It is meaningful when he has sufficient control to be able to use the power according to his own designs. It is meaningful when, through its application, the manager can produce a substantial increase in profits and performance through his own efforts.

When the manager must decide when and how to use authority, on the basis of his own initiative and knowledge, the authority has substance. When there are few, if any, convenient excuses for his not using the authority, and when there is no one else to whom he can turn for a decision, or blame for having advised him wrongly—the authority has substance. The impact of such authority lies in the realization that it is a lonely kind of power. It is the power a man uses according to his own judgment in a situation in which he is aware that he stands alone in bearing the prime responsibility for his actions.

A production supervisor in a food–processing plant found himself in just such a situation. On his own initiative, he realigned the duties of the personnel on his production line in a way he anticipated would increase his output. Soon after, his production went down. He looked outside his own group for the reason—or an excuse. He found nothing to blame, although he was sure the decline was not his fault. He sought advice from engineers on the department staff, but they could not offer a solution. He had just about determined to revert to his previous alignment, when he decided to examine his line again. As a result, he found the bottleneck that caused the problem, and corrected it with a simple change. The productivity he had anticipated was achieved.

The lesson here is that a pattern of authority that prevents a man from being fully responsible for his decisions, or inhibits him in recouping from unfavorable results caused by his decisions, is something less than effective. Power should be distributed in such a way that a man has the authority not only to make decisions, but to recover himself from erroneous or inadequate ones.

The pattern of authority should be susceptible to continuous change. It is quite unrealistic to settle on a given pattern of authority and regard it as a permanent one. Of course, there are some general concepts that may be long-lived in that they express the basic philosophy of how the organization is to be managed. This could include, for example, the policy that the company is organized and operates on a centralized basis. But even such a fundamental policy should be open to evolutionary change. Another concept that could be considered to have some degree of permanence is the authority relationship between the board of directors, the president, and an executive committee. Nevertheless, with regard to most aspects of the pattern of authority in a company, there seems to be little benefit in thinking of them as unchangeable, by reason of the excellence of the pattern at the time it was devised, or for any other reason.

The fact is, changing circumstances necessitate revisions in the pattern of authority, if its effectiveness is to be maintained on a continuing basis. In any case, the pattern does change under the pressure of events, even though management may not become aware of the change for a while because of administrative inertia.

Officials in the corporate headquarters of a nationally known group of department stores were proud of the cost effectiveness of their concept of centralized procurement of merchandise for all outlets. In recent years, the company had followed the general trend of establishing suburban stores outside large urban centers. As suburban operations expanded, the sales volume of style merchandise in these branches began to show a profound weakness. Corporate headquarters finally concluded that the suburban store managers were right in their protests about the merchandise that was being shipped to them, sight unseen. They had been claiming all along that they should have strong and independent roles in the buying function, in order to meet the unique demands of their individual markets.

In this case, top management recognized that a change in the pattern of procurement authority was needed, because of the impact of different buying habits in various suburban areas. Fortunately, corporate officials really believed in a flexible approach to doing business. Therefore, each branch manager was given the power to have a voice in the purchase of style merchandise for his store.

The pattern of authority does not have to be strictly compatible with the organization structure. As indicated in earlier chapters, management often views the delegation of authority as a complementary and subsidiary aspect of the official organization structure. It is usually accepted as a process whereby those who occupy the various "blocks" in the organization chart are given the license to carry out their assigned functions. So the delegation of authority is, to some extent, an automatic action that goes along with the initial design of the company structure and any subsequent changes to it. In actuality, the authority structure follows the organization structure only up to a point. As we have seen, it has a life of its own. It can be so vibrant that the real power structure sometimes takes its shape from the pattern of authority rather than vice versa.

The pattern of delegated authority should be generally compatible with the organization structure; that is, some degree of deviation between the two is acceptable (but only for a period of time). It is usually true that if the pattern of delegated authority is changed by management, it is wise to make an appropriate accommodation in the organization chart, or in functional assignments.

In contrast to delegated authority, acquired authority is often generated and exists in a form that is in no way visualized in the formal organization structure. This does not mean that it is completely incompatible with the structure as dictated by management. Acquired authority is more often neutral, rather than contradictory, in the framework of the formal organization structure. For example, acquired authority can arise in areas not specifically covered by the formal organization, because the tasks or relationships involved are not understood or anticipated. Thus acquired authority either grows in the gray areas between the defined segments of the organization, or it spreads out adjacent to, and beyond, the scope of the formal organization. Of course, the company must always be alert to the growth of acquired authority that does, in fact, contradict the formal organization. Then, a decision is needed as to whether it should be cut short or recognized and adopted as being better than the authority pattern based on the formal organization. The principal thought in this guideline is that management should not insist that the exercise of power must always strictly conform with the existing organization structure. Such insistence tends to inhibit, rather than improve, the pattern of authority.

When the nature of authority changes for the better, the change should be recognized officially whenever possible. The dynamics involved in the use of authority often cause specific segments of it to become different from, and better than, those originally envisioned by management. This process is certainly true of acquired authority (as discussed earlier), and even occurs in the normal course of the application of delegated authority. When a beneficial change occurs, and the new configuration of authority is accepted by management, it should be legitimized (whenever possible) in the same way officially delegated authority is sanctioned.

Official recognition of new authority is a way of rewarding the manager who had the courage and foresight to develop it. Perhaps even more important, it prevents loss of the continuing benefits that would occur if top management did not give its official sanction. Productive power, once identified, should be added to the "list" of official authority so that it can become a permanent asset.

The exercise of authority should be related to high performance. Management should make known its support of this principle through the practice it follows in both delegating authority and rewarding excellence in its use. The idea that authority represents a unique means for high accomplishment is thus emphasized. It is a power that produces results. Inert authority is a waste; it is the cause of negative performance.

With just a modest investment of effort by management, the relationship between effective use of authority and high performance can be made visible by giving stature and recognition to those who use power in a fruitful way. The mere act of publicizing meritorious performance of this kind, even at a moderate level, serves to spread the idea that authority is a real and living force in the organization. For a far greater impact, we can move from this modest approach to a considerably more advanced program for relating authority to an expectation of high performance. At that level, we find a sophisticated and very modern concept of delegating authority. It is based on the idea of deliberately delegating authority in terms of achievement of managerial objectives. This approach (discussed at length in the next chapter) is referred to as results-oriented delegation of authority.

Identify those areas in which it would be beneficial to upgrade the application of authority. Typically, some functions and departments in the company produce greater benefits than others from a liberal and in-depth use of authority, whether delegated or acquired. In view of this fact, it is often profitable to adopt a selective approach in encouraging the use of authority. In areas in which a more intensive use of power would be highly beneficial, management should be willing to endure a reasonably high risk of error that might result from ineffective use of expanded authority. Also, it should be willing to put more thought and effort into planning for a broader and deeper use of delegated and acquired authority.

The kinds of places in the company in which it would be beneficial to upgrade the application of authority are the areas in which:

□ It is evident that limited results are being achieved because competent supervisors are fearful, for some reason, of operating with vigorous leadership.

□ It is apparent that many decisions that should be made at lower levels are being passed up the line.

□ A high degree of managerial creativity would pay substantial dividends that are not currently being realized.

□ The rapid development of managerial talent is important.

□ It has been demonstrated, or is evident, that a substantial volume of undistributed authority exists that can be put to work for the benefit of the company.

Having identified those selected areas in which an expanded exercise of authority would be most beneficial, management should then proceed to encourage that expansion by the most appropriate means available.

Delegate and permit acquisition of authority according to the competence of the individual manager. There is no rule that says all managers must be treated equally in terms of the extent and quality of authority they are allowed to exercise. This is true even where the organization structure (or any other form of basic policy) appears to indicate that two or more positions should rate the same degree of authority. It is management's prerogative to permit differences in power, depending on the relative competence of the individuals in those positions. In fact, two successive incumbents of the same position might well have different levels of authority because of their differing capabilities. Thus the personal qualities of the individual can often have a profound influence on higher management's decision as to the authority pattern in his position. In personnel circles, this is referred to as *the man in the job* concept.

Not everyone is capable of exercising a substantial degree of authority. Supervisors who are excellent in other managerial traits may sometimes be better employed under a grant of authority that is narrower than would be expected in a given position. Other managers who are deficient in some respects may consistently be highly successful in terms of gaining benefits through the application of an extensive degree of authority. Personal traits and attitudes are factors to be weighed in deciding on the degree and quality of authority that a manager is allowed to exercise.

Maintain awareness of the actual pattern of authority. There are several important reasons why management should be aware of the real distribution of power in the company at any given time.

□ It helps management to know whether or not authority and responsibility assignments have been made for the entire range of functions visualized by it as being necessary.
□ It provides a capability for immediate identification of who is to be held accountable for what.
□ It provides management with a ready indicator of the best organizational location for assignment of new actions, programs, or functions that it wishes to undertake.
□ It provides information for decisions about hiring, promoting, training, and paying managers and other personnel, in accordance with the needs of the company and the skill and effort required in each position.
□ It aids the boss in identifying those subordinate managers who should be controlled more closely than others in regard to their exercise of power.

The need to know the real pattern of power applies equally to both delegated and acquired authority of any standing. As we shall see later in this chapter, there are many means readily available to management for keeping aware of the distribution of authority.

Establish controls to provide a warning of actual or potential misuse of authority. Obviously, a balanced approach is needed in creating a good atmosphere for the effective use of authority, delegated or not. Management is always hopeful that authority will be used beneficially and within the bounds of good reason. However, although many men may be deemed worthy of using delegated authority, it is to be anticipated that a few are going to use the authority wrongfully. It must be acknowledged that this possibility of misuse of power is especially significant in cases where there is a permissive attitude toward acquisition of authority. (Some basic methods for setting up controls to warn of possible misuse of authority are discussed later in this chapter.)

Make specific assignments of functions down to the lowest level of supervision. Many companies do make functional assignments to some, if not all, levels in the organization. Ordinarily, however, they tend to be quite general, especially at the first-line supervisor level. The significance of assigning a specific set of functions to each person in management is that:

□ It provides a solid base on which to evaluate a manager's use of available and potential power.

□ It encourages supervisors to extend their scope of authority because they can move into nearby undefined areas without trespassing into someone else's delegated area of authority.

□ It provides the basis for a supervisor to demand that a peer do something he is responsible for, so that the supervisor can exercise his own authority.

When an individual manager is given a "charter" as to his specific functions and duties, he is on his first step away from a feeling of impersonality—a condition that can be frustrating in a company of any size. He now has grounds for thinking of himself as a partly independent operator. He can shed the feeling that he must look frequently to his superior to be told what to do next. The manager knows that he is responsible for specific functions and that he has the authority to carry them out. Favorable attitudes of this kind promote a feeling of independence, and motivate the manager to acquire whatever legitimate authority is needed to do the job.

A cautionary note about this technique: If company management definitely will not accept the spread of authority beyond the limits of assigned functions, it is probably better to state the functions in broad terms. Specifically defined functions can be like leg-irons when the atmosphere is unfriendly to acquired authority.

Broaden the supervisor's responsibility for implementation of changes suggested by him. A common situation (which dampens initiative in the exercise of authority) is the existence of limitations on the supervisor's responsibility for carrying out those actions he has decided upon for himself. The man who has the authority to make, but not to implement, a decision is bound to suffer from stifled initiative. In many organizations, there is a deliberate fragmentation of responsibility and authority to the extent that the man who makes a decision is often forced to look up the chain of command to give effect to his decision.

In this day of specialization, it is seldom regarded as beneficial to have an organization in which any one man carries out a wide range of tasks and functions. (Recently, there have been some second thoughts about the validity of this theory, based on findings of behavioral scientists. Currently, considerable research is being done regarding the advantages of "job enrichment," an approach that includes broadening the range of tasks assigned to a man or a group.) In any case, various means can be used to involve middle- and lower-level "decision makers" in a wider span of actions resulting from their decisions. This can be done, for example; by giving the manager a voice in the method and schedule to be followed in carrying out the actions he inspired. Or he can be provided with the opportunity to oversee and coordinate the action taken by others in implementing his decision. Also, feedbacks can be provided to him, showing the progress of implementation and the results of his decisions.

Anything that can be done to deepen a man's involvement in, and knowledge of, the results of his own decisions provides him with a sense of participation in matters that are important to the company. The basic aim is to prevent a man from feeling compartmented into a small, highly defined area. If he is permitted to step out of this area in key situations, he can better visualize the connection between his decision and the end result that is important to the company.

Evaluate and rate managers on the basis of their proficiency in delegating authority and encouraging assumption of it. This head-on technique is not aimed at those who exercise a given body of authority but, rather, at their bosses. It is a means of involving everyone in the executive and supervisory ranks as missionaries in the effort to encourage a beneficial pattern of authority. This approach provides an incentive to those who are in a position to delegate authority, or who can encourage subordinates to assume it, to do so in a proficient manner. The method is initiated by informing all managers that they are going to be evaluated on their performance in this regard. Such evaluation can be carried out within the framework of a performance rating system, in judging the suitability of managers for promotion.

Proficiency in delegating authority can provide some interesting benefits to managers. In a certain large western banking conglomerate, a senior vice-president attributes his swift rise in eminence to his practice of consistently delegating almost every bit of his authority to competent subordinates. It seemed, to his principals, that he was always available to take on the special and important projects that other executives were too busy to handle. He always made sure that these extra assignments were done well, since he was in a position to devote a substantial amount of personal attention to them. His principals always noticed his successes in these tasks. They also became aware of his proficiency in finding subordinates who could carry the load of his regular duties. (This executive, incidentally, is still successful in his special technique for getting ahead.)

The foregoing twelve guidelines cover a wide segment of the types of action that can be taken to improve the pattern of authority. The remainder of this chapter is devoted to a more detailed discussion of two of these guidelines, which merit further exploration: *keeping aware* of the current pattern of authority, and *maintaining control* of it.

Keeping Aware of the Authority Pattern
The need to know how power is distributed in the company applies to both delegated and acquired authority. Manage-

ment should know who is doing what, and how these actions fit into the desired pattern of authority. It is especially important that management be in a position to determine whether or not instances of acquired power are acceptable, as measured by the company's organizational concepts and goals.

If management accepts the idea that authority should be exercised outside the confines of formal delegation, it must anticipate that acquired authority will spread out in many directions. Just as the tendency of a plant or shrub to spread can be controlled by careful cultivation, the proliferation of undelegated authority should be controlled by careful management. The pattern of growth and change must be kept under observation.

With this concept, we now have a complete rationale for the use of administrative power as a medium for the growth of the company and its individual managers: First, distribute authority in a formal manner to provide a firm foundation for the continuing operation of the company; next, encourage the use of authority; then, permit it to grow beyond the official bounds that have been set down; finally, be aware of how it spreads, and guide it when it threatens to go outside acceptable limits.

Before establishing specific methods to maintain awareness of the power structure, it is important to determine where and how the resultant information is to be collated and analyzed for top management's benefit. If there is a specialist on organization matters on the company's staff, his is the logical place for this task. He is already aware of the formal organization and distribution of delegated authority. Also, he has probably established good channels of information for other purposes. The task would be a reasonable extension of his duties.

If there is no one in the company who is regularly involved in organization development as a full-time or part-time task, the job of monitoring the authority structure can be assigned to a high-level staff person or administrative assistant as a collateral task. Another option is to assign it to an appropriate senior executive for performance within his group. A logical candidate would be an official in charge of a service function (rather than an operation), such as the controller, the head of the administrative department, or even the personnel manager. In any case, the individual selected for this work should be in a position to have sources of information that go down into the organization, as well as direct access to higher officials in the executive power structure. Very often, people in the upper reaches of management are in a position to provide early and significant information about changes in the authority pattern.

Discussed below are some of the individual key sources of information that should be monitored to detect what is occurring in the authority structure of the company. At this point, some readers may have misgivings about the ethical considerations involved in these types of monitoring. Others may feel that an unfavorable managerial backlash can result from this kind of observation. Actually, these techniques for gathering information are really systematic methods whereby management can carry out one of its basic, recognized responsibilities—control. If the company climate is such that any manager could conceivably regard this type of activity as spying, or in some other unfavorable light, then management should certainly widely advertise the facts about its program of observation. The effectiveness of the methods described here in no way depend on secrecy or underhandedness.

The key sources of information for keeping track of the authority structure are:

Sample the channels of communication. The observer of the power pattern should take advantage of a primary characteristic that exists whenever authority is in the process of change—that is, the authority a man has, or seeks to acquire, is usually meaningless until it involves other people inside or outside the organization. From this involvement of other people arises the need to *communicate* with them in some manner. (In some cases, the modification or acquisition of power may not involve other people so much as *machines*. But again, some form of communication is necessary in order to put power into effect.)

Whatever form for interchange of information exists, it provides a channel that can be observed and monitored (usually on a sample basis) to detect changes. The most basic kinds of communication in this category are organization charts, functional statements, job descriptions, statements of company policy, procedure manuals, and the like. Above this very basic level, one of the most productive types of communications is what is sometimes called the reading file. Many companies have a requirement for retention of file copies of nonroutine correspondence between departments of the company and with outside sources. The reading file is a collection of these copies in one package, which is available for higher–level review on a periodic basis, before the copies are permanently filed. This type of communication frequently reveals how delegated authority is being exercised, and also divulges situations in which someone is going beyond the bounds of formally delegated authority.

Other communication channels (depending on company practice) suggest themselves readily to the observer of the authority structure. With experience, screening such sources for this purpose can be carried out quickly by an occasional review.

Use information from management audits. Another conventional means for learning about changes in the authority pattern is to utilize the internal audit program that exists in some form or other in many companies. Generally, the purpose of such audits is to check compliance with established procedure and company policy, to recommend improvements in company systems, procedures and practices, and the like. This form of management survey frequently turns up a wealth of data regarding deviations from the formal pattern of authority. Auditors may find situations such as these: Functions or services not planned by management are being performed; actions are being approved at levels not normally authorized to do so; or procedures are being carried out in a manner other than that previously directed.

The personnel who perform management audits and reviews can be instructed to report on any deviations or variations from standard practice that management is not already aware of and has not previously approved. The reports should include an evaluation of the benefits and validity of such practices.

Use information from reviews of organizational structure. If the company has an established system for reviewing organizational structure and functional assignments, these reviews can be utilized for monitoring changes to the authority pattern. This type of program may take the form of a series of surveys of various departments, for example, or it may incorporate a continuing review of changes in job descriptions. In any case, in these areas of auditing, changes in the approved authority structure frequently surface at an early period. An alert observer can detect unplanned variations from the pattern of delegated authority by reviewing the results of the program.

Analyze management information. A very useful means for maintaining awareness of the authority pattern is by the analysis of management information. Any primary reporting system that a company has for the regular submission to top management of operating, budgeting, or other financial data can provide clues on many types of changes involving the exercise of authority. For example, a review of unforeseen changes in the expenditure of funds in specific accounts could lead to a determination that money is being spent in a way not normally expected to result from the regular application of authority. As illustrated in the case described below, an analysis of key operational statistics can provide similar clues.

The Operations Review Board of a medium-size manufacturing firm, in reviewing quarterly management statistics, found that sales of a particular item had taken a sharp upward trend in the most recent quarter. Since no one in the group was aware of anything that would account for this, it was earmarked for investigation by the Board's staff. Investigation showed that the increase resulted from the initiative of the sales manager in charge of this item. He had gathered data that convinced the production manager and a staff man in the controller's office (who was the principal adviser on sales discounts) that long production runs of the item would result in drastically lower unit costs. The three men agreed that a special discount structure was justified for very large volume orders of the item. On this basis, the sales manager was able to offer a significantly better price than competitors for large orders, and sales on the item jumped.

Although the sales manager had not requested official approval of the discount, the investigation showed that company procedures did not specifically require such approval, and the Review Board was satisfied that the man had used proper discretion in the use of his acquired authority. In taking action to set up the special discount rate, he had checked with the best sources available to him—that is, the proper production manager and the adviser in the controller's shop.

The Board noted that the gross profit from this exercise of acquired authority was very substantial. It also found that this particular sales manager had moved into other open areas of authority, in that he had prepared and mailed advertisements to all actual and potential buyers of the item involved, telling them of the special discount structure. Furthermore, he had instituted a similar review of other items in his list to determine if there were other good candidates for special discounts.

As a result of the Board's interest in the matter, the company established a new policy for identifying high-discount items. Sales and production managers were encouraged to submit suggestions on products whose characteristics would permit various beneficial changes to be made in price and sales features. The new system also provided for funneling such suggestions through an approving authority at the sales department level.

Where a company has a management reporting system of some type, the vigorous pursuit of clues offered by such data can provide an insight into the changing pattern of authority. Another example of useful management information exists in companies that have a system for reporting departmental progress toward previously established goals or objectives. Such systems offer a particularly useful source for tracking changes in the pattern of authority. When a target is set, and some form of recognition or reward is related to accomplishment of it, managers are naturally motivated to seek unusual ways of achieving the target. Often, the methods employed to move toward the goal include the use of initiative in such a way that some degree of change in the authority pattern is likely to occur.

Virtually any system of performance evaluation of managers offers a source of information about power patterns. The evaluation process necessarily involves an examination of the manager's mode of operation. Something is revealed about what he has been doing, and how he has been doing it. Most forms of performance appraisal, therefore, offer an opportunity to bring to light those occasions in which a man has been using his initiative to do his job, including instances where he has moved beyond his delegated authority.

Keep an ear to the ground. There are many ways in which an observer can become aware of modifications of authority, or exercises in the use of undelegated authority, that are self-initiated by managers. The everyday flow of communication between officials, the luncheon talk about business, the casual discussion of what happened yesterday —all provide information on this topic. There is the plain fact, too, that the exercise of authority by a manager has a certain degree of visibility because it almost always involves someone else in the company.

Another visibility–producing factor in the use of authority (acquired authority, especially) is that, usually, no great effort is made to keep it completely secret. Normally, when a man takes his first tentative steps toward using a new segment of acquired authority, he is discreet and quiet about it. He may even attempt to mask his actions in order to avoid undue initial attention. But having taken a series of steps toward putting into effect the newly gained authority, he seldom has reason to hide the legitimate benefits that have resulted from his initiative. An effort to maintain secrecy would be inconsistent with the reasons that ordinarily motivate a man to acquire authority. It is a truism that authority must ultimately be displayed in some fashion in order to be effective.

The most likely instances in which a continued effort would be made to hide the use of authority are those in which the user feels some guilt about what he has done, or suspects he will be criticized or penalized if his actions are found out. In some circumstances, if a great effort is made to maintain secrecy, the use (or misuse) of power can be kept hidden for a long time. But the very effort to keep it hidden robs it of its effectiveness. Where criminal intent is involved, such as in the case of unauthorized handling of funds in order to promote personal gain, the normal procedures of internal financial auditing, or similar security measures, are usually effective.

In summary, it can be said that it is not difficult, for those in management who need to know, to maintain a continuing knowledge of what is happening to the authority structure. Time and effort are required in the process, but the means to do it are readily available. As a complementary action to the encouragement of legitimate use of both delegated and undelegated authority, knowledge of the changing structure of authority not only is highly useful but is virtually essential.

Maintaining Control of the Authority Pattern
Obviously, the distribution of authority is anything but a yes-or-no proposition. Many shades of delegated and acquired authority are to be found in modern practice. Of course, some limitations on the use of authority are firmly fixed, but beyond these primary controls, other limitations vary under different conditions. In fact, there are so many combinations of control and permissiveness, many of which are extremely subtle or obscure in their implications, that gaining knowledge about how any one company handles its distributed authority is a study in itself.

Despite these fine distinctions in the art of controlling authority in the organization, some basic facts can be stated. In general, most controls can be categorized into two general types: first, those that are predetermined—fixed and essentially unchanging limits on authority; second, those that are tailored to specific situations (often developed as a result of a boss's awareness that a subordinate is moving in a certain direction in his exercise of authority).

An examination of current practice shows that there are nearly always fixed limits on authority (of the first type described), even when a man is given full responsibility for something. A line manager may well wonder, for example, what degree of real authority has been delegated to him when he observes that he is hedged in and limited by an ever widening assignment of authority to his functional and staff counterparts. Particularly in the program manager concept, the tendency in technically oriented companies is to superimpose program management authority on existing organizational formats. The limitations on the scope of authority of the regular line supervisor that result from this arrangement are obvious.

Although the manager may feel harassed by the fixed limits placed on his authority, some basic minimum level of controls is definitely necessary. Certain conventional types of limitations on delegated authority exist widely, especially those placed on the administrative actions of supervisors. Some common restrictions are: a limit on the power to make capital expenditures (no more than $1,000 in any one transaction, and no more than $20,000 a year, for example); a limit on the power to adjust salaries (no adjustments that take the salary above $400 a month, for example); a limit on the authority to discharge an employee (often, the immediate supervisor has no final authority at all to fire a subordinate). Limitations of this kind are usually reasonable in principle. In practice, however, they sometimes represent an unnecessary imposition that is out of context with the authority the manager actually has. As a case in point, there is a manager of a retail store, which is valued at $2 million, who is allowed to spend up to $100 on equipment without prior approval!

In the predetermined, fixed category of controls, top management frequently sets down a series of rules that apply across the company. Beyond this, it is sometimes necessary for a departmental boss to establish additional predetermined and fairly permanent guidelines on the use of authority by his own subordinates. He has a wide range of choices, but he must make up his own mind about the degree of flexibility to apply. Obviously his fixed limits can be structured to vary from manager to manager and from situation to situation. It is not proposed here that the boss be told how to structure his predetermined limits on authority.

However, it may be useful to consider a brief description of several levels of control, any one of which a boss can specify for the guidance of his subordinate managers, beginning with the most liberal level.

1. Take action as determined necessary; no further contact with me is needed.
2. Take action—but then let me know what you did.
3. Look into the problem, then:
   a. Let me know what you intend to do. Do it unless I say no; or,
   b. Don't do it until I give approval; or,
   c. Let me know the alternatives, with pros and cons, and your recommendations; or,
   d. Let me know the facts; I will then determine the alternatives and decide on a course of action.

Consider now the second general type of authority controls—those that are tailored and variable according to the specific situation, or the individual manager. This type is often designed on the basis of the feedback information that results from monitoring the manager's actual use of delegated or acquired authority. The information gained from being aware of the actual use of authority, as discussed earlier in this chapter, provides an excellent basis for exercising this type of control.

The types of control a boss exercises in this category mainly reflect the level of guidance he wishes to provide as to how power should be exercised in specific situations. In a sense, then, this category of control is more a matter of training than of policing. It is undesirable, of course, to impose impediments that make it impossible for the manager to use authority in an imaginative way. At the same time, the boss must be alert so as to eliminate the chance for independent use of authority in a manner that can cause unacceptable losses. Thus the boss seeks to control the individual use of power in a manner that will produce a suitable balance. His managers may use authority to the extent that it is profitable or otherwise beneficial, but the risks of improper use of authority must be kept to a minimum.

In regard to the use of tailored controls, it is not possible to state specifically how authority should be governed in relation to a given set of circumstances. However, here are some general principles that can serve as guidelines for action.

(1) Consider the optimum situation, in which a principal is capable of exercising personal control in such a way that he achieves exceptional performance from his managers. Under these ideal conditions, a subordinate shows high performance when he has independence in pursuing his own work, and, at the same time, sees his boss often. A boss's active interest in his subordinate's current work, combined with a hands-off policy in regard to directing it, is an effective way to encourage and control progress by subordinates. This is not always easy for the boss to do, because if he keeps in touch with progress, he is naturally inclined to impose his own ideas. Here, we see the heart of the problem in controlling authority, even under optimum conditions. Having once delegated the authority, the boss should allow the subordinate to work out his own destiny. At the same time, he must remain in touch with the situation to the extent necessary to exert control of it when required.

(2) When the ideal situation does not exist (which is usually the case), it is probable that control is required because one or the other of these two conditions exists to some degree: underutilization of available power, or overutilization of authority to the point where it can be harmful to company operations. In other words, the most active forms of control are dictated by either too little or too much use of authority.

Where there is too little use of authority, the principal corrective action by the boss should take the form of encouragement. He should point out to the manager those specific instances in which action could have been taken. The more specific, detailed, and personalized the boss's guidance is in these cases, the better. He can go as far as helping the subordinate actually use the authority in several "live" situations. Having worked with the manager in a real-life manner, the boss is in a position to discuss and exemplify the various techniques for using delegated and acquired authority. (It can be particularly helpful if the boss reviews with his manager the techniques for acquiring and using authority that are discussed in Chapter 5.) In this way, by practice and precept, the manager who is low in authority utilization may get some ideas through the encouragement and guidance given him by the boss.

(3) When the boss determines that there is an inordinate degree of overexercise of power by a subordinate manager, a series of actions can be undertaken.

First, the boss should instruct the manager regarding the correct manner in which to use power. He should stress that the acquisition and use of authority is not bad in itself; in fact, it can be a definite advantage to the company.

Second, once a manager has transgressed beyond the acceptable use of power, his boss should keep a close check on him. If the manager again moves too far from his functional area, the boss can detect the action quickly, possibly on a before-the-fact basis. If the manager persists in overextending himself beyond the wise and proper application of power, he can be enjoined from using any authority beyond that specifically delegated to him. Such a restriction can be imposed on a temporary basis, until the manager gives evidence of having gained a sense of perspective on the matter. If he does not learn this, some form of permanent action is indicated.

Last, when such a manager, who has been in difficulty because of overutilization of power, shows evidence of having come back into line, he should be praised and recognized for carrying out those correct actions. Complimentary evaluation of performance is also an effective method to use in cases where a manager has corrected his *under*utilization of authority.

9 * USING AUTHORITY TO GET RESULTS

Excellent results can be attained in practically any business climate through effective distribution and use of authority. Some situations, however, are more favorable than others for inspiring in company officials the conviction that authority is an asset capable of producing notable benefits. A favorable climate exists, for example, where *management by objectives* is employed as a means for stimulating high performance by supervisors.

The use of performance objectives is perhaps the most dramatic and successful approach for the "management of managers" to have appeared in recent decades. In this method, specific and quantitative targets are set for each manager. His subsequent performance is then appraised in terms of achievement of these targets. Besides motivating individual managers to exceptional levels of performance, the technique produces many other distinct benefits, not the least of which is that it helps managers to gain an enlightened vision of the role of personal initiative.

Performance objectives provide a direct and highly visible link between the manager's personal aims and the company's goals. This kind of intimate company/manager relationship offers a welcome opportunity for the manager to acquire and use authority in a way that will expand his view of his personal power in the organization.

This chapter discusses the very interesting concept of

performance objectives for managers, including the methods that can be employed for distributing authority in the light of targeted results. Major attention is given to use of these methods in situations where the company has no established program of performance objectives (since this is the more prevalent situation). Of course, this approach can be conveniently incorporated into an existing program of performance objectives.

AUTHORITY IS NOT AN END IN ITSELF

No company is in the business of delegating and using power for its own sake. There is no profit in building authority as an end product. Whatever business the company is in, authority is a tool it uses to achieve its purposes. Therefore, authority should be delegated and regulated in a manner that serves the best interest of the company—that is, in a way that enables the organization to meet its goals.

A company's goals can be projected down the organization structure and, thus, ultimately be expressed as a set of personal objectives for each manager. The manager's objectives are related to his own assigned functions. When the individual manager achieves his objectives, the company as a whole moves a little closer to its goals. But to accomplish this, the manager needs his share of power. In this sense, therefore, a manager's authority can be defined as the power he needs to meet his objectives.

By establishing personal objectives for the manager, individual authority assumes a meaning consistent with the most significant fact in the life of the organization—the achievement of company goals. Authority becomes a living aspect of management. It is not based on a frozen concept of the company's functions. The organization's goals vary and change from year to year, or for even shorter periods, and the scope and meaning of every manager's authority change with it. Because power is tied to results, rather than solely to a fixed matrix of functions, the pattern of authority necessarily takes on a viability and flexibility that brings it close to the realities of company life.

DEVELOPING MANAGERIAL OBJECTIVES
IN TERMS OF COMPANY GOALS *

To illustrate how performance objectives for managers are developed, we consider very briefly the steps carried out by a boss who is intent on using them for his subordinate managers. His first step is to determine the company's goals. These goals state what the company hopes to achieve in a coming period, such as a year. Goals are often described in statements prepared for stockholders, directors, or top management. When they are not, information on them is usually available from executives at higher management levels, or from company departments involved in planning, budgeting, management analysis, or the like. If such sources cannot provide adequate information, the boss may have to develop a set of goals that are appropriate and challenging for his own department.

Company goals are usually stated specifically and in quantitative terms. They relate principally to sales, profits, return on investment, and other unmistakably important measures of company progress. Ordinarily, they do not convey a sense of being easy to achieve, for they are a challenge to greater company performance. So we find such company goals as: (1) increase by 50 percent or more the sales volume of the ten products that showed the highest profit margins last year; (2) reduce by 20 percent the average sales cost per unit of each item the company has been selling for at least three years.

Once company goals are determined, the next important action is to spell out the direct relationship that exists between these goals and the job of the individual manager. This process begins when the manager and his boss jointly agree on a small number of clear statements (perhaps four or five) delineating the essential functional responsibilities of the manager's position. Next, the relationship between each function and a pertinent goal is written out in words that are specific and meaningful in everyday terms. For example, consider goal (1), stated above, regarding an in-

---

* This process is described in detail in the book *Performance Objectives for Managers* (AMA, 1966) and the recording "The Goal-Setting Session" (AMA, 1967) by the author.

crease in sales volume for high-profit items. The company's advertising manager and his boss agree that one of the manager's functions is to carry out advertising campaigns that promote the company's special sales programs. The relationship between this function and goal (1) is expressed as follows:

> The advertising manager is to select promotion themes, media, and display methods; to develop scripts and layouts; and to coordinate advertising campaigns to stimulate increased sales of selected high-profit items.

This statement of relationship is further refined into a generalized objective for the manager, a description that expresses what is to be achieved. To make the objective more pointed and specific, a quantitative yardstick is added to it—a means for expressing even more precisely what is to be achieved by the manager. It also provides a basis for measuring his progress toward the objective. The end product is a performance objective for the manager, such as:

> The advertising manager is to use 20 percent of the annual advertising budget to promote the sales of selected high-profit items. The effectiveness of the sales promotion media and methods used will be such that readership response will be 50 percent higher than the averages achieved last year, as measured by the response indexes usually employed.

The result of this process, then, is a set of specific managerial objectives that tie the manager's functions to the company goals and express his targets in a quantitative, understandable, and challenging way.

A basic requirement for success in the use of performance objectives for managers in that the boss and his subordinate manager develop them jointly. In that way, corporate goals are personalized for the manager by himself, with the guidance and assistance of his boss. The manager knows now that this is his "baby." These are his objectives, and he is more inclined to attempt to achieve them than to quarrel about their precise validity. Thus, personal objectives become a significant motivational factor for higher performance.

MANAGERIAL OBJECTIVES ADD REALITY
TO AUTHORITY

Performance objectives for managers are not a guarantee that delegated and acquired authority will always be used in a highly effective way. Nevertheless, the use of managerial objectives can be extremely helpful in making authority real and meaningful to executives and supervisors down the line. As stated earlier, objectives serve to connect the manager's actions directly to the basic purposes of the organization. Moreover, since the manager has participated in describing his objectives, and they are his own objectives, he at least has some feeling of independence and some flavor of being in business for himself.

Performance objectives are planned on a medium-length time base, such as a year. Therefore, the manager does not feel an obligation to make repeated reports to his boss about what he is doing, for the purpose of reassuring the latter that he is not going beyond the bounds of his authority. In this concept, the boss is not concerned with giving orders daily, nor is he a super decision maker who has the last word on every decision his subordinate makes. He acts as a supporter and guide, offering advice, helping in problem definition, and providing the resources needed by subordinate managers. In effect, he concentrates mostly on managing the environment in which the managers can grow rather than on controlling these men. Experience has shown to an overwhelming extent that the manager becomes very fond of the idea that he has the responsibility and authority he needs, and that the boss is not always looking over his shoulder to check on his actions.

When authority is tied to results, it provides benefits that are not easy to come by in other techniques aimed at motivating managers. This approach eases the manager's feeling that he must conform to specific limits of authority and responsibility. He has greater freedom to express his individuality and independence of spirit in taking action to reach his objectives. Risk taking is encouraged, and the limits can be clearly defined by the manner in which objectives are stated. The assignment of objectives also tends to eliminate the yes-man syndrome—a prevalent condition where authority is closely held and company goals are poorly understood. When authority is tied closely to objectives, it is an aid in rapidly identifying the occasional incompetent manager.

All in all, the building of a bridge between personal objectives and the use of authority serves to humanize and personalize the organization. This relationship between personal ambition and the use of power is compatible with what has been learned in recent years about human needs and behavior. The use of results-oriented authority tends to strengthen the individual manager's competence in a way that is consistent with the company's need to make a profit.

To sum up the manner in which managerial objectives add reality to the exercise of power:

□ *The manager's authority is based on what he can achieve in his position,* as expressed in quantitative and objective targets that are directly related to key goals of the company.

□ *The use of objectives tends to maximize the range and depth of the manager's authority* in relation to his responsibility as a member of management. He is in a position to create objectives or services that are the distinct products of his own efforts.

□ *Authority tied to personal objectives helps to push power down the organization structure.* Supervisors have greater responsibility for their results and a greater degree of authority to make the decisions needed to attain such results.

DISTRIBUTING AUTHORITY ON A
RESULTS-ORIENTED BASIS

In most organizations, there is no company-sponsored program of performance objectives for managers. Let us examine now, starting from scratch, how a system would be developed for delegating authority on a results-oriented basis. Assume that the approach is going to be used within a department of a company, under the department head's sponsorship, and with no particular assistance from outside his own area. Since this is the most common situation that might be encountered, a discussion of it should help bring into focus the essentials of this approach.

At this point, we consider the question of how much time is involved in the process of setting targets for the individual manager, then defining his authority in results-oriented terms. An extensive period of time is not usually required, when measured in light of the benefits to be expected. In any case, whatever the time expended, it will pay dividends —even if the sole result is an improved understanding on both sides as to what is expected of the manager, and what his responsibilities and duties are.

Moreover, this process often *saves* time. As a result of the clear statements of functions and authority, time is saved that would otherwise be spent in defining them whenever questions arise in regard to day-to-day problems.

In this description of the process of distributing authority on the basis of achievement, there are three phases:

1. Develop performance objectives for the manager.
2. Develop a statement of the manager's authority as it relates specifically to his performance objectives.
3. Develop a separate statement suggesting potential avenues that the manager can explore in order to acquire authority. (This is an optional step.)

Developing Objectives

Phase 1 in the process was described earlier in the discussion of how performance objectives for managers are developed. To summarize the steps: Company goals are identified, the manager's functions associated with these goals are determined, and then, managerial performance objectives (with built-in yardsticks) are developed. Thus the end product of the first phase is a description of the results that are expected of the manager within a given future period (such as a year).

It is only fair to say that this specific approach for developing objectives is by no means the only technique available. The concept, however, has been used successfully by many companies. The principal requirement is that some methodical approach be used to define in specific terms the results expected of the manager. Preferably, whatever method is used, the results expected from the manager's performance should be:

☐ Linked directly with the principal functions of his position and the known goals of the company (or, at least, the goals of the department).
☐ Stated in quantitative terms. The target should be set at a challenging level which, if achieved, indicates that the manager's performance has been excellent.
☐ Determined on a joint, participative basis by the manager and his boss.

Here is an example of an expected result that was developed by a shop foreman and his boss, for the foreman. It is related to a production department goal, aimed at improving product quality. The expected result was:

On an annual basis, 97.5 percent of the units produced will be accepted by inspectors on the first pass, and the cost of scrapped units will be maintained at less than one percent of the total manufacturing costs.

Note that this objective (or expected result) is specific, quantitative, and directly connected to the manager's principal tasks, as well as to the department's goal. It is also noteworthy that it was set at a substantially higher level than has been previously experienced.

Stating the Manager's Authority
In phase 2 of this process, the boss and the manager develop a statement of the latter's authority as it specifically relates to each expected result (or performance objective). This statement is not intended to be a comprehensive description of the manager's authority. It does not replace any basic delegation of authority granted to the manager through normal avenues, such as organization charts, job descriptions, or company directives. Rather, this results-oriented statement of authority should supplement and explain more definitely what the manager already understands to be

his delegated authority. It is a specific and enlightening statement of authority as related to results or objectives. Normally, this process provides new insight into the exact nature of the manager's power.

In developing a results-oriented statement of authority, there are certain guidelines as to what to include and how to state the authority.

Express a direct connection between each objective and the manager's authority.

Be as specific as possible, and include examples, if necessary. Use everyday terminology that is familiar to all concerned.

Include in the statement of authority, whenever appropriate, any definite limits that should be made known to all involved, so as to provide a better understanding of the delegated authority.

Define the scope of the particular kind of authority, as well as the depth to which it extends. For example, suppose a manager's statement of authority indicates that he has the power to requisition tools or equipment to assist his subordinates in maintaining products within certain tolerances. It would also be appropriate to state the total dollar value of the items he is authorized to requisition in a given period.

Exercise special care to avoid conflicts or overlap of authority between managers.

With these guidelines in mind, we examine some excerpts from the results-oriented statement of authority developed for the shop foreman mentioned earlier. The foreman is authorized to:

□ Requisition (without higher approval) tools, equipment, devices, or services—whatever support is needed to assist his subordinates in achieving quality targets—up to an amount equivalent to one percent of his total shop costs, on an annual basis.

□ Negotiate with inspection supervisors on matters relating to quality control standards and techniques. He is authorized to jointly approve, with a qualified representative of the inspection department, those changes to quality standards that are accepted by both parties as not adversely affecting the operational and maintenance capabilities of the product, as defined by the engineering department.

The example shows that it is quite possible to be definite and specific about the nature and extent of the authority that relates to the accomplishment of expected results. It should also be observed that the kinds of authority being delegated to the foreman are not of a minor nature.

Suggesting Possible Acquisition Areas
Phase 3—an optional one—in the process of distributing authority on a results-oriented basis moves the manager and his boss into interesting territory. In addition to the statement of delegated authority discussed above, a separate statement can be developed to suggest the possible avenues and directions the manager can explore in order to *acquire* authority. This procedure is not essential for achieving benefits from the results-oriented approach already discussed. Much can be gained even if this third phase is not attempted. Nevertheless, it is a very useful technique in itself, in cases where the boss seeks to encourage a subordinate's use of initiative. If there is some reluctance about undertaking the risks involved in this technique, the definition of potential acquisition of power can be deferred until after some experience has been gained with the basic approach of stating only delegated authority.

The method used for describing the potential areas for acquiring authority should be tailored to the manager's attitudes, skills, and personality; that is, the possible sources of acquired authority should be predicated on the man rather than the position, although the authority should obviously be related to his functions. Furthermore, the statement of potential acquired authority need not be spelled out in the detailed or specific terms employed in describing delegated authority. It is, of course, very helpful to use clear and unambiguous language. Also, initially at least, the suggested avenues for acquiring authority should be more modest than revolutionary. The principal aim is to stimulate the manager's initiative by offering him advice as to directions in which he can go, particularly those appearing to have high potential for benefiting the department.

With regard to the foreman in our case, here is an extract from the statement describing his possible avenues for acquiring authority:

□ Contact the engineering department and discuss with engineers: (1) the possible actions you can take to eliminate the most common types of errors that result in producing units that do not meet quality standards; and (2) the validity of certain quality control standards that you doubt are meaningful in terms of acceptability of the product.

□ Contact customers and inquire whether or not the presence of certain "defects" in the product would really be unacceptable to them.

□ On a trial basis, use your favorite methods to rework pieces rejected in inspection, as a means of reducing scrap losses. Carry out such trials even if company inspectors, engineers, and accountants have predicted the methods will be unacceptable.

A final feature in the techniques for distributing authority on a results basis is the use of an effective follow-up procedure, a means for periodically checking on progress toward expected results. An advantage of using performance objectives is that progress reviews need not be conducted through frequent direct observation of the subordinate's use of authority. Instead, periodic discussions on progress are held by the boss and his subordinate. The intent is that the discussions, in themselves, will reveal how the authority is being used, what attempts have been made to acquire it, and whether or not the use of authority is helping the manager move toward his objectives. The focus should be on results and achievement of high performance. A discussion every few months will provide an unobtrusive control and guidance feature. Also, there are opportunities for periodic adjustment of targets and authority statements, as well as for further coaching on the acquisition and use of authority.

DISTRIBUTING AUTHORITY VIA AN
ESTABLISHED OBJECTIVES PROGRAM

The discussion just completed applies to the distribution of authority on the basis of results in cases where the company has not previously established a performance objectives program. Where such a program is already in being, it is relatively simple to extend the system to cover authority assignments. All that is required is to carry out the second phase (developing statements that relate authority to the objectives) and, if desired, the third phase (suggestions for acquisition of authority). The general approach covered in the last section is perfectly applicable here. No other revisions need be made to the existing performance objectives program.

AN EXAMPLE OF RESULTS-ORIENTED AUTHORITY

This case illustrates the overall approach to distributing authority through the use of performance objectives. Bill Evans is the head of the purchasing department in a division of a large corporation that manufactures electronics products. Bill's division makes parts and components that are used in a wide range of electronics products, from small radios to large computers. The division's output not only is used in the assembly of final products made by other divisions of the company, but is sold to other manufacturers. Bill's department buys everything from raw material to finished parts, products, and services, for use in his division's manufacturing and administrative operations. He reports to P. R. Vickers, a senior vice-president of the division.

Mr. Vickers and Bill held several discussions about the latter's performance objectives and the authority they considered necessary to the accomplishment of these objectives. Listed below are three of the objectives jointly developed by Bill and his boss. Under each objective are listed a few of the statements of delegated authority agreed upon. Also shown are some related areas of potential acquired authority that Mr. Vickers suggested Bill might wish to explore as an added means for achieving the results indicated in the objectives.

OBJECTIVE 1:   Reduce the purchase department's cost to buy, per dollar of goods or services purchased, by 12.5 percent.

Delegated Authority.   You are authorized to:

a.   Initiate firm recommendations to reduce the average number of employees in the department to the extent considered appropriate.

b.   Modify the resources for which you are charged in departmental overhead burden (space, equipment, and so on).

c.   Revise internal processing methods in such a manner as to produce improvements but not affect the procedures of other departments or the character of the purchasing department's outputs.

Potential Areas of Acquired Authority

a.   Contract with an outside consultant firm to review the department's operations for opportunities to reduce expenses. The maximum amount authorized to be paid to the consultant is $6,000.

b.   If it is determined that substantial portions of the cost to buy are based on factors outside the purchase department, attempt to influence other departments to modify their actions so as to reduce their impact on the cost.

OBJECTIVE 2:   In order to secure more competition and lower prices from suppliers, increase the number of companies on the list of potential suppliers by 35 percent; at least half the commodity groups under which suppliers are categorized will show an increase in the number of qualified suppliers.

Delegated Authority.   You are authorized to:

a.   Divert a reasonable amount of the department's resources to research efforts for enlarging the list of suppliers.

b.   Contact industrial, governmental, and other sources to develop leads on additional suppliers.

c.   Develop improved methods for acquiring new information about potential suppliers.

Potential Areas of Acquired Authority

a.   Place ads in appropriate trade magazines, soliciting

potential bidders to submit information about themselves.

b. Attend industrial conventions and meetings to become acquainted with potential new sources.

c. Make personal visits to other companies to exchange ideas on the development and maintenance of the suppliers list.

OBJECTIVE 3: Improve substantially the quality of technical information used in making purchases for at least 75 percent of the items that account for half the total procurement dollars expended annually. The evaluation as to whether or not substantial improvements have been achieved is to be made quarterly by a senior engineer from the corporation staff.

Delegated Authority. You are authorized to:

a. Negotiate regarding technical information requirements and standards with other departments that supply the data, such as engineering and production departments.

b. Develop file data requirements that will insure immediate availability of technical information when purchases are to be made.

Potential Areas of Acquired Authority

a. For some selected pilot items, develop optimum data packages (better than those presently received) and use them for test buys. Determine which types of data packages will improve procurement factors in any way, such as an increase in bidders, lower cost, faster delivery, and the like.

b. Report directly to supervisors in other departments any lapses and errors in technical data supplied by those departments.

With this set of objectives, descriptions of delegated authority, and suggestions for acquired authority, Bill Evans had a much better picture of where he was going, and how he could use his authority to get there. Mr. Vickers mentioned to Bill that they would get together every three months to discuss Bill's progress toward the targets stated in his objectives.

RELATIONSHIP AMONG MANAGERIAL
OBJECTIVES, INITIATIVE, AND AUTHORITY

At this point, it should be evident that the effectiveness of applied authority varies according to the use of initiative by the man having that authority. Both delegated and acquired authority can encompass a great deal of power that often goes untapped, unless initiative is applied in its use. The setting of objectives or targets for a manager can be a key method for igniting the application of initiative via the medium of authority.

The great benefit of defining authority in terms of results is that it clarifies that often foggy knowledge of just what the manager can do in his job. The reason is that the objectives help to focus attention on concrete and quantitative targets, which in turn throw light on the power that can be used to achieve them. Thus the definition of expected results makes it possible for the manager to understand his authority at the same level of perception that he has regarding the everyday requirements of his job.

THE IMPACT OF RESULTS
ON AUTHORITY CONCEPTS

From the standpoint of management, the definition of authority on the basis of results and managerial performance can have a rather profound and favorable effect. This approach provides a medium for tying in the exercise of authority to some very significant factors: the goals the company seeks to reach on a short and mid-range basis, and the capability of the individual manager to achieve high performance in relation to those goals. It is certainly a departure from the more classical and abstract notion of delegating authority to a position because of its location in an idealized concept of the company's organization.

Any program that defines and encourages the use of authority in terms of results desired by the company, and in relation to the individual manager who is going to contribute to these results, can have a lasting effect. Its impact will be felt on the authority concept in the company, and on the way in which authority is exercised in actual practice. Where this approach is used in an organization, and where it is producing favorable results, management should be quick to reinforce it. This can be done by: officially recognizing the effective use of authority to achieve good results; giving permanent status to acquired authority that has been used well; and continuing to push forward the boundaries of every manager's authority. Even where there is a vigorous results-oriented program, it will nevertheless take a long time to use up all the potential authority inherent in the company. There is so much of it that is untapped.

INDEX

143